AIM SMALL, MISS SMALL

Answering the Call to Spiritual Maturity

MARK HASENYAGER

xulon PRESS

AIM SMALL, MISS SMALL
Answering the Call to Spiritual Maturity
by Mark Hasenyager

Printed in the United States of America

ISBN 9781498424073

www.xulonpress.com

CONTENTS

◎

Part 4: Balanced Priorities

Part 5: Godly Character

Part 6: Sacrificial Service

INTRODUCTION
◎

Desert Storm was the first war of my generation. It happened so fast and seemed to be so one-sided, it was hard to think of as a war, but it was; lives were lost and survivors were changed forever as they dealt with what happened. Prior to Desert Storm I had learned and heard a lot about the Vietnam War: a war that went on way too long and tore our country apart, leaving everyone with the depressing feeling that no one really won. There is such a difference in those two wars; it is hard to even put them in the same category.

Without trying to offend anyone, if I had, had to go to war, I would have rather been in Desert Storm than the Vietnam War. Give me clear targets and sure weapons, so the fight may be swift and victory certain. When your life is at stake you don't want to be on the losing side, nor do you wish to be in the conflict for an extended period of time. Without clear goals and victories we find ourselves losing hope. When the enemy is unknown, confusion between who can be trusted and who we are fighting against takes hold, and we find ourselves fighting against ourselves.

We as believers in Christ are at war, a war that contends for the souls of everyone around us. As a believer you are on the winning side, but I believe the church across America is fighting a 'Vietnam War'. There are no clear goals for victory, as to how we are to live our lives as a believer. We do not understand the schemes of the enemy, and we find ourselves fighting battles that do more harm than good. The weapons we are using lack the power of God to demolish strongholds; they tend to be the newest and latest ideas that worked for someone else, but are really only the teachings of men, lacking the true power to change us. That sounds a lot like the Vietnam War to me.

God has laid out clear objectives in his Word for us to have victorious lives in Him. My prayer is that this book will provide you with a battle plan outlining the objectives for spiritual victory in the Bible; so you can tap into the power of God which brings victory to you and glory to God

ACKNOWLEDGEMENTS
◎

First and foremost I have to thank my incredibly patient wife. Not only has she helped me with this book, the ministry I've done throughout my life would not have been as rich and rewarding if she was not my true partner. People who know us know she is the real reason anything I do succeeds.

My three girls who are the love of my life; I'm very proud of the life they live for Christ. They have molded me from a boy to a gentleman. Writing this book took a lot of time and they have been a great encouragement through the journey. Hannah, I love your tender, nurturing, heart, and your passion to love people, who are on the edge, to Jesus. Naomi, I love your consuming desire for God and your passion to serve. Rebecca, you bring such joy to life; I love how God has used this joy to reach others.

To our "adopted family": Chelsey, Andrew and the Hunt families, you are an incredible addition to our family; we are blessed to have you. It blows my mind that you would choose us to be with, but what a gift it has been. Our shared memories are some of the greatest in my life.

I have been blessed with many mentors throughout my life. Steve Scranton who hung out with a confused teenage boy whose family was falling apart and reassured me that God had not left me. Dave Foster who gave a young man a chance at youth ministry, taking a bigger risk than most would ever do, because he believed God uses the underdog. For Bob Bland who taught me leadership, sometimes by fire. To my close friends the Beeman family who loved and believed in me; you have been a true gift to our family and I am forever grateful.

In the last few years Dave Howeth and Doug Hutcheson have been my mentors and in many ways they have encouraged me to train and help other church planters. Their incredible insight and wisdom has laid the foundation for Multiply Northwest.

I can't say enough about Heather Hunt who not only puts up with my requests, but literally translated my dyslexic mess into English so this book could be published. To Kim Houlihan, an incredible gift, who has put in many long hours painstakingly editing every letter of this book. To Paul Hunt, who has been a vital part of processing the principles of this book and is my true Timothy in ministry.

To the good people of Outdoorsmen Church who have loved, encouraged and supported a somewhat crazy elk hunter in his call to serve the Lord.

To the entire Multiply Northwest team who have patiently waited while I wrote and coached them at the same time.

This book could only have happened because these people allowed God to work through them to influence me. My wish is, this book will influence my grandchildren, both physical and spiritual, to come; that they may know what it is to live a life sold out to Jesus.

PART 1:

SPIRITUAL MATURITY

Chapter 1

SPIRITUALLY MATURE OR SPIRITUALLY RETIRED
◎

*For if you possess these qualities in increasing mea-
sure, they will keep you from being ineffective and
unproductive in your knowledge of our Lord Jesus
Christ.* 2 Peter 1:8

My wife and I had been in ministry together for thirteen years when God called us to plant a culturally
relevant church in the mountains of Montana; what an incredible ride it has been. We have had the privilege of seeing God
draw in the lost and hurting through our doors; watching
them build trust with Christians, become curious to the point
of desiring life change, and finally surrendering themselves
to God has been some of the greatest moments in our years
of ministry. It has been such a thrill to see new believers and
their passion and hunger to know the Word of God. Watching

as they discover that God's word is alive and active, and not only does it apply to their life, but it will transform them inside and out, has been life changing; not only for the new believers, but for us as we partner with them in this journey.

If you have received Christ as your personal savior, what were you like as a new believer? Were you curious, did you hunger to know more? I think we all did. It is part of being born again. A toddler hungers to learn and experience all they can of the world; to hear, smell, touch, taste and feel everything, much to the horror of new parents. As new believers we experience rebirth, we are new creations. We should be like toddlers hungering to know and grow more, and I would say, if there is no hunger at the beginning, there probably was not a true beginning.

Eventually, we all grow older and after a decade of ministry in our new church, it saddens me to see what 'growing up' looks like for so many believers. Many have lost their passion for the Word; they have come to act as so many 'older Christians' do. They know the Word just enough to no longer hunger for it; their knowledge has grown, but they no longer apply it to their lives. Their service to the community becomes obligation versus passion. Where once they prayed believing God for big dreams, now they pray passively not believing God will truly act.

It breaks my heart that so many once hungry and passionate believers come in time to a place where they believe they are spiritually mature, yet, what I have seen is their maturity is not maturity at all. Instead it's as if they have become spiritually retired. Instead of a close, vibrant faith, believing God for incredible things, they are having a "seen it, done it...nothing new under the sun" kind of living. As Timothy writes they are "having a form of godliness but denying its power;"[1] I believe many live in quiet desperation longing for something more.

I know God wants something different for us; we are not just on this earth to survive, but to thrive in a personal relationship with Christ, attractive to unbelievers; Not just going through the motions, but living a day to day victorious life, hand in hand with our Maker, which is the purpose of this book; bringing people regardless of where they are in their spiritual walk back to a place where they are spiritually thriving.

Chapter 2

THE PETER PAN MENTALITY
◎

Instead, speaking the truth in love, we will in all things
grow up into him who is the Head, that is, Christ.
Ephesians 4:15

I'm concerned that as you begin to read this book and see the words, spiritual maturity, you will mentally tune out. Most of us would agree, to mature is good, but there is a side of us that doesn't want to grow up. As Peter Pan says, "To live will be an awfully big adventure."[2] We would rather live free, adventurous lives, being young at heart rather than dealing with the pressures and responsibilities of being an adult.

"It takes *courage* to grow up and become who you really are."–E.E. Cummings (emphasis added).[3]

Before I became a father I was an uncle. How I loved riling my nephews up before bedtime. I'd buy them cheap dollar store swords, and we'd play for hours in hay stack forts we'd created. I'm glad to say, when I became a dad, I did not put away my childish ways; I will never regret the hours we spent playing and adventuring together as we make crazy memories.

One of my relatives once told me how glad she was to see how much I had matured. At first I was pleased, but then I came to realize that her measuring stick was not even close to my own. When I saw how she measured maturity, I decided that like Peter Pan, I didn't want to grow up either. If growing up means just sitting around drinking coffee all day, no thanks; as Jesus said, "I have come that they may have life, and have it to the full."[4]

So often we see maturity as limited and boring, to take the fun and passion out of life; however, true spiritual maturity is freedom, adventure and the fullness of life we were made for. To lack it is to miss out on what life could be, to live your life incomplete. Let's face it; there is nothing that makes us want to grow up more than spending the day with someone who is immature. Being around their self-absorbed lives makes us determined not to follow in their footsteps; it makes us feel sorry for them because they are missing out on what life could be. Without becoming mature and complete, we mess up and miss out. All of us long to be better, to not be lacking; we long to get life right.

Not long ago I sat down with a good friend, who started coming to church one year earlier, to talk about discipleship. Being a new believer, I wanted his insight. I asked him why he thought it was so hard for people to enter into a one on one mentoring relationship, which in my experience is the backbone of effective discipleship. I thought he would say something like its intimidating or something like that.

He hesitated before he answered,

"You're not going to like this, but why? Why would they want to meet with someone? What benefit is there to something like that?"

He was right; I did not like what he said at all. The answer my friend gave reveals the heartbreaking reality of my church, and many of the churches I have been around. The church has not done a great job of discipling its people to a place of victory in their lives. If we had, people would not be questioning the benefit of discipleship; the benefits would be seen in us as we are growing and living out the life Christ calls us to.

I believe most of the Western world struggles with what discipleship is, because we don't know what we are aiming at. Growing up in the Northwest, hunting has been a way of life. God has given me the privilege of harvesting some incredible animals, but my wife still thinks my biggest trophy is the mouse I shot through the ears with my bow. In the movie, *The Patriot*, Benjamin Martin tells his young sons as they aim their rifles,

"Aim small, miss small".[5]

How can we achieve something we do not shoot for? As older believers we know we are commanded by Christ to make disciples and to teach them, but no one has modeled it for us; we struggle to hit the mark, because we don't know what we are aiming at, other than wrestling with the frustration that we are supposed to be progressing spiritually, but how?

"Without vision the people perish."[6] When I don't have a goal — no aim, I become lazy. Satisfied that I'm ok, and don't need to push forward.

Without an effective understanding of what it is to be mature, Christians often look no different than the world. Though many ought to be teachers, the majority don't even understand the whole gospel. True discipleship ought to bring about spiritual maturity, exemplified by total life change.

According to a study done by Barna Group with Living on the Edge; we are missing the mark entirely. As a result of their study they discovered that: *most churchgoers are not clear what their church expects in terms of spiritual maturity* (emphasis added).

An open-ended survey question asked churchgoers to describe how their church defined a "healthy, spiritually mature follower of Jesus." Half of churchgoers simply said they were not sure, unable to venture a guess regarding the church's definition. Even among born again Christians — that is, a smaller subset of believers who have made a profession of faith in

Christ and confessed their sinful nature—two out of five were not able to identify how their church defines spiritual maturity. Among those who gave a substantive response, the most common responses were having a relationship with Jesus (16%), practicing spiritual disciplines like prayer and Bible study (9%), living according to the Bible (8%), being obedient (8%), being involved in church (7%), and having concern for others (6%).[7]

This confirmed God's leading in my heart to help believers measure, develop, and experience the blessings of spiritual maturity as defined by God's word. Because, as my friend pointed out, without understanding the great benefits of what a discipleship relationship brings to his life, who would enter into the disciplines that it requires?

The Bible quite obviously mentions the concept of spiritual maturity on several occasions; verses such as: "Until we all reach unity in the faith and in the knowledge of the Son of God and become mature, attaining to the whole measure of the fullness of Christ. Then we will no longer be infants, tossed back and forth by the waves, and blown here and there by every wind of teaching and by the cunning and craftiness of people in their deceitful scheming" (Ephesians 4:13-14); clearly states it is the responsibility of church leaders to help believers mature spiritually. As leaders of the church we need to clearly define what it is God asks of us, and how to attain a spiritually vibrant life.

As the leader of my family I have the responsibility to help my children become mature. I've always been the easy-going parent and nothing much ruffles my feathers; that is until my kids started to chew with their mouths open. I couldn't stand it but for some reason it didn't bother my wife at all. What did bother her was how I was bothered every time we had dinner as a family. Finally she came up with a solution. We have always tried to add humor to our discipline and to let the punishment fit the crime. Her solution, the next child who chewed with their mouth open got their entire meal blended, since they weren't mature enough to eat solid food. Sure enough the next night, the roast dinner was blended for the offending child. I must say it was highly effective and all three of my daughters were 'cured' that day. I could also recommend this as a diet plan; none of us felt like eating again for days.

> "In fact, though by this time you ought to be teachers, you need someone to teach you the elementary truths of God's word all over again. You need milk, not solid food! Anyone who lives on milk, being still an infant, is not acquainted with the teaching about righteousness. But solid food is for the mature, who by constant use have trained themselves to distinguish good from evil" (Hebrews 5:12—14).

The writer of Hebrews rebukes the letter's recipients because of their lack of maturity. Note he says "trained themselves," in other words, they pursued something which changed their life and brought about maturity. And again 1 Peter 2:1-3 says, "Therefore, rid yourselves of all malice and all deceit, hypocrisy, envy, and slander of every kind. Like newborn babies, crave pure spiritual milk, so that by it you may grow up in your salvation, now that you have tasted that the Lord is good;" Peter encourages new believers to mature and crave to grow.

Some years ago I led a group of people from our church to Bryce Canyon in Utah, to hike down into the Hoodoos. These formations are some of the most beautiful and mysterious canyons I have ever seen. After visiting the overlooks many times I was thrilled at the opportunity to go deeper into the valley and truly discover the wonders of the valley.

We packed up and drove through the night from Missoula, Montana. That morning when we stopped for breakfast we all downed a lot of coffee in the hope of staying awake for the remainder of the trip. Making it to the trailhead around noon, we quickly grabbed a trail brochure and headed down the path during the hottest part of the day. Some of the guys had 80 pound packs, no joke, we weighed them, but we were absurdly confident. We had backpacked together for years in Western Montana, how could the desert be anything different?

The first 100 or so yards in, we were offered spectacular views. As we descended further down into the canyon we discovered the best views of the Hoodoos were from the parking lot. By the time we got to the bottom of the canyon we couldn't even see the Hoodoos. The hike down into the canyon was steep and arduous with little hope of finding water; the description of Bryce Canyon as a high plains desert had escaped my attention while we were planning this trip, but now as we hiked in, it had become glaringly obvious.

Everyone had gone through most of their water before we were a third of the way down; by two-thirds of the way down the situation was getting bad. I have been in some hairy situations before, but this one had me concerned. Not the least of which was because our three little girls were with us, and everyone was becoming dehydrated. It was too late to turn back; there was no guarantee of water ahead.

Finally we found a small trickle of water. To say we craved water at this point would have been an understatement. We were beyond thirsty, and literally sick. We spent the rest of the night laying around nursing each other back to health.

I think the American church is in the same place we found ourselves at the bottom of that canyon: We know what we want to see as believers, but many of us don't know how to achieve it; we don't even know where we're headed. We have loaded up our fellow believers, and ourselves, with heavy packs of spiritual disciplines. We want to grow deeper in our faith and experience the victorious life God wants for us, we go to church each week, do Bible studies, go to conferences, but we end up continuing to fill our packs with, "I must do this, and stop doing this." We end up even further from what we wanted to see in our lives and our real spiritual thirst is not satisfied.

Even though the Bible often discusses spiritual maturity, it is still widely misunderstood. The two most common misunderstandings being:

1. The idea that spiritual maturity is following all the rules and becoming spiritually disciplined.

The Barna Group and Living on the Edge also found in their spiritual maturity study that: *Most Christians equate spiritual maturity with following the rules* (emphasis added).

One of the widely embraced notions about spiritual health is that it means "trying hard to follow the rules described in the Bible." 81% of self-identified Christians endorsed this statement, and a majority agreed strongly (53%). Even among those individuals defined by their belief that salvation is not earned through "good works," four out of five born again Christians concurred that spiritual maturity is "trying hard to follow the rules."[8]

Spiritual discipline is another term we hate, and probably with good reason. I know marriage is work, but if you tell me I need to discipline myself to spend more time with my wife, it would turn my relationship with my wife into drudgery. Rather than longing to have the best possible relationship with my wife, to pursue, invest and love her deeply, life would become full of must dos, compared to a life of passionate pursuit of my wife.

2. The idea that spiritual maturity is manifested by knowledge.

These misconceptions run the risk of leading people to faithfully attend church, adding to their knowledge of the Bible, and of God, but never experiencing true life change. Sadly, these individuals often become proud and judgmental, because of the time they've spent adding to their knowledge. In the end, they look a lot more like the Pharisees than Jesus, holding to rules about behavior instead of experiencing life transformation. Much to our shame, the world looks upon these misled individuals and concludes that Christianity has no real value.

Simply stated, to become mature is, to become like Jesus Christ. "Rather, clothe yourselves with the Lord Jesus Christ, and do not think about how to gratify the desires of the flesh" (Romans 13:14); "My dear children, for whom I am again in the pains of childbirth until Christ is formed in you" (Galatians 4:19); "Follow my example, as I follow the example of Christ" (1 Corinthians 11:1).

To become like Christ means, every part of our being must change to be like Christ. It is not enough to focus solely on our knowledge of Christ or Scripture. If our primary goal is to obtain knowledge, we are more apt to become like a Pharisee than like Christ. The early church in Antioch had very limited access to gaining knowledge, but according to Acts 11 they were the first to gain the name Christians, literally little Christ.

It's important to note, the time we have been a Christian is not a true indicator of our development. More likely it acts to reveal where we lack. Just because your child spent a year in school does not mean they are ready to move on to the next grade. During the year, they should have learned what they needed, but time is not a measure of growth; their grades are. So, why would we think time would be the proof of spiritual development?

On more than one occasion I have witnessed a longtime Christian, claiming to know their Bible inside and out, say something that revealed their heart, one that was so anti-gospel I was tempted to make a whip and drive them out of the church. What makes me mad about these individuals isn't that they messed up, but rather they believed they'd arrived spiritually and were proud about it, and yet their heart revealed they were not a reflection of Christ at all.

Chapter 3

GROWING UP
◎

For physical training is of some value, but godliness has value for all things, holding promise for both the present life and the life to come. 1Timothy 4:8

God often gives us physical examples to help us understand spiritual principles. So, let us compare our spiritual maturity to our lives. Personal maturity is not restricted to a single area of life; rather, it is measured by our physical, emotional, social and mental state of being, in conjunction with our age. Although some characteristics of development are out of an individual's control, most are learned behaviors which are developed, or hindered, by inside and outside influences; coupled with our personal desire to further ourselves.

To clarify, I do not claim to be a professional in psychology; I do believe I am a student of people, because of my position in ministry. I have a desire to figure out how personality, culture, and upbringing influence how we process life and who we eventually become.

I have observed emotional maturity is trained and developed primarily by our family influence; especially by our parental influence. Our sense of love, security, and self worth are primarily developed early, some emotions for the good and some which we must later learn to overcome. Social maturity is developed directly by the people we are exposed to. The greater the range of age groups, social classes and cultures we're exposed to, the greater our social maturity can become. Mental maturity is developed through the things we are taught, as well as by what we seek to learn. Our physical maturity is developed by the environment in which we live coupled with our desire and the social pressure around us to be healthy or not.

When the tennis player, John McEnroe, who should act as an adult, throws a tantrum like a preschooler, it is an embarrassment and source of irritation. There are many movies out there which use the embarrassment of immaturity as a form of comedy. It is hard for me to believe they have made yet another sequel to *Dumb and Dumber*.

On the other hand, immaturity brought about due to a physical or mental disability often brings heartache, because of the opportunities such impairments will prohibit.

There are those who struggle socially. They want friends or a mate, but have no idea how to engage in or carry on a conversation without making it awkward. Often these people have great hearts, but they are socially immature due to insecurity.

As a youth, I could hold my own; no one seemed to intimidate me. Many adults commented on my maturity, which I now realize was my ability to communicate comfortably with them. But, somewhere along the line, when I became a pastor I became intimidated by my peers. I feel at ease with everyone from the homeless to successful CEOs, but put me in a room full of pastors and I can't get a word out straight. I feel small, inadequate. I believe this is due to my feeling of inadequacy as a teacher. One of the most frequent comments I get as a preacher is how encouraged people are because, if I can do it they should be able to too. I am thankful God has used my lack of schooling and inadequacies to encourage others, but just because we are used despite of, or through our failings doesn't make it any less humbling.

An adolescent may be considered physically mature because their body has undergone puberty, however, due to sitting around or bad eating habits their body may be far from physically healthy, which is an aspect of physical maturity. Alternatively, someone who has trained and developed their body to be above average exhibits great physical maturity, which is something to be desired by all, regardless of age. Just think about how many people watch the Olympics.

I've matured beyond the desire to obtain to the level of a professional athlete's fitness; the temptation for me now is like Paul Terry said, "Whenever I get the urge to exercise, I lie down until it goes away."[9] But, to be honest I push through because I highly value being fit enough to enjoy the great outdoors to the fullest.

How we develop and mature affects the way in which we live our everyday lives. In the same way, it shouldn't be hard to believe our spiritual development affects our ability to experience what God desires for us. Furthermore, our spiritual maturity has a direct impact on our personal development.

Sometimes the effects of an immature individual are really only felt by those close to them. In ministry it is so hard to watch those who are immature, but have no passion to change. Often we offer classes on getting victory with finances, marriage and family investment in the hope of helping certain people gain victory; they refuse to come. The classes are usually attended by those who are already fairly healthy.

On the other hand there are those who know they struggle and sincerely desire life change, but don't know how to even begin. The benefits of spiritual maturity are considerable, as Paul said, "For physical training is of some value, but godliness has value for all things, holding promise for both the present life and the life to come" (1 Timothy 4:8).

The truth of the matter is we will never experience the promise of a victorious life until we grow in our faith. I believe this is partly what Jesus meant when he said he came "to give us life and life more abundantly."[10] This life will impact our self-identity, our relationships, our career, our wisdom and our knowledge; it is the key to peace, joy, and purpose. It will bring victory over worry, sin and the things which plague us. It will not only bring us to the knowledge of

God, but will lead us to experience His power and presence on an increasing scale in our daily lives.

It may seem like these are lofty claims, but they are not my own. These promises are for you, through Christ, in God, when you believe in God's power. His Word, the Bible, holds the truth to bring change and purpose to your life. Jesus, His son, died for your sins and through His resurrection and the power of the Holy Spirit, you too are raised and given new life to overcome this world.

Who wouldn't want to take part in all the Bible has promised? It is essential to understand many of these promises can only be experienced as we develop and grow in our spiritual maturity.

Chapter 4

THE POWER FOR LIFE CHANGE

◎

[We] must believe that He exists and that he rewards those who earnestly seek him. Hebrews 11:6b

My eldest daughter struggled with speech; even at five years of age she could only be interpreted by her younger sisters. As often happens they picked up on her speech patterns and behaviors, and by the time they entered school they all needed speech therapy. Unfortunately the patterns were very difficult to break. Our girls are adults now, and they still trip up from time to time. One day, not long ago, one of our daughters hurt her thumb. She cried out,

"Owww! I hurt my fumb".

As we started to laugh, she got mad and said,

"What, do I need speech ferapy?"

I'm truly not trying to pick on my girls, (they won't believe me) but, those we surround ourselves with deeply impact our development. We tend to try and fit in; to conform and copy others. We see this play out in many areas of our lives. The longing and desire to fit in, to conform, and copy others drives the fashion industry and fuels our economy. Those who are surrounded by the wealthy tend to eat better, read more books and be more driven to succeed. A study done in 2014 shows Montana has the seventh lowest BMI (Body Mass Index) in the nation.[11] Why, because we are surrounded by people who are passionate about being as healthy as possible, to enjoy our Big Sky country to the fullest.

If we are highly influenced by our friends and neighbors lifestyles and choices, it only makes sense they would also have a tremendous impact on our spiritual development as well.

The problem with immaturity is we often don't see it in ourselves; it is generally only recognized by those who are more mature than us. We grow as we learn from and are taught by those around us who are more mature.

For believers, this guidance is found first and foremost through the Holy Spirit. The most important key or foundation for a vibrant spiritual life is the presence of the Holy Spirit; without whom no one will ever become mature and complete. As a matter of fact, pursuing maturity without the Holy Spirit would result in our becoming spiritually immature, because our pursuit would be by our own merit rather than the changing and renewal by the Holy Spirit.

A toaster is truly only functional when it is plugged in to its energy source. I can't think of any use for a toaster without power. I understood this more fully after staying with my in-laws for a few weeks; they unplug everything immediately after using it. I spent days frustrated because my toast won't toast, the kettle wouldn't heat, etc. It drove me crazy until they explained why. One day they closed the cabinet over the toaster and inadvertently pulled down the lever, resulting in a melted wall. Thereafter, everything was kept unplugged.

If our end goal is to become more like Christ we cannot hope to do it without His Spirit. We would be like an unplugged toaster. It is the work and power of the Holy Spirit which transforms us. "For who knows a person's thoughts except their own spirit within them?"[12] Jesus told us the Holy Spirit would become our teacher, guide, and companion; as well, our prayers would be answered only because the Spirit is with us. All the key areas of Spiritual growth come only through being in step with the Holy Spirit. There are going to be areas of needed change which only the Holy Spirit can reveal to us. Sometimes these areas are revealed by the power of the Holy Spirit working through others, but only as you seek Him and the truth. Even still there are some things that will only come in His timing and will only be revealed as we experience life transformation.

Peter is a great example of how the Spirit and someone used by the Spirit revealed his immaturity. Paul gives an account in Galatians of his confrontation with Peter over the way he was acting around the Jews who had a hard time accepting the Gentiles.[13] Also, in Acts we see Peter's conception of the Gentiles being challenged through a vision given him on the roof.[14]

Pursuing spiritual growth in our own power, without the Holy Spirit, leads to pride and religious structure. Paul warned against this:

> "So then, just as you received Christ Jesus as Lord, continue to live your lives in him, rooted and built up in him, strengthened in the faith as you were taught, and overflowing with thankfulness. See to it that no one takes you captive through hollow and deceptive philosophy, which depends on human tradition and the elemental spiritual forces of this world rather than on Christ" (Colossians 2:6—8).

"Since you died with Christ to the elemental spiritual forces of this world, why, as though you still belonged to the world, do you submit to its rules:

> 'Do not handle! Do not taste! Do not touch!' These rules, which have to do with things that are all destined to perish with use, are based on merely human commands and teachings. Such regulations indeed have an appearance of wisdom, with their self-imposed worship, their false humility and their harsh treatment of the body, but they lack any value in restraining sensual indulgence" (Colossians 2:20—23).

In other words, the change they experienced came from religious practices and self inflicted rules rather than true victory which is only accomplished through the work of the Holy Spirit. Therefore, before we pursue spiritual maturity, we must first be sure of the Holy Spirit in our life.

To understand the Holy Spirit is a lifelong pursuit, but there are some basics to know and experience. Some teachings of the Holy Spirit differ from denomination to denomination, but all evangelical churches agree the Holy Spirit empowers believers not only to live according to God's Word, but also, He brings new life, to be reborn.

The Holy Spirit is known as the third person of the Trinity, and is God. His responsibility is to dwell within believers as the seal of God, claiming them as His own; He teaches, and reminds believers of Christ's words, He intercedes on the behalf of the believer, He makes known God's will and plans, He rebukes when the believer steps out of line, and He is known as the great comforter. The Holy Spirit produces the fruit of Godly Character when the believer stays in tune with Him. Sounds pretty important, doesn't He? Well, He is. He is only available to those who repent of their past sins, accept in faith the grace Christ gave on the cross, and surrender their new life to God.

The Holy Spirit will empower or fill us to do things beyond ourselves. However, this won't happen frequently until we are maturing spiritually. This does not mean the Holy Spirit does not dwell in us all the time, but there will be times of incredible awareness of His presence.

More than once people have come up to me after my sermon; their demeanor ranging from perturbed to downright angry, crying out,

"How did you know? Who told you? I don't get it. How did you know exactly what I was going through this week and what to say?"

At first I was taken back, wondering what on earth they were talking about. But then I realized it was just that the Holy Spirit was filtering what I was saying to what people were hearing in the sermon; exactly as they needed to hear it. Often people have told me of something which had profound impact on them that I never planned on saying or even remembered saying. As a pastor I am so thankful the Holy Spirit is working despite me!

It is possible to quench the voice of the Holy Spirit. If we continually do something which does not align with God's will, or when we set our desires over God's, the power of the Holy Spirit is held back and even silenced by our unwillingness to walk as God has called us. I believe this is what it means to be out of step with Him.

As we further discuss the process of spiritual maturity, it is with the understanding, the Holy Spirit is the one who empowers and strengthens us through the process. Therefore as we journey towards spiritual growth, we will be asking the Holy Spirit to teach, lead, correct and rebuke us.

Chapter 5

DEFINING SPIRITUAL MATURITY

◎

Don't let anyone look down on you because you are young, but set an example for the believers in speech, in conduct, in love, in faith and in purity. 1 Timothy 4:12

The Bible refers to several characteristics of spiritual maturity such as the verse above; "But the fruit of the Spirit is *love, joy, peace, forbearance, kindness, goodness, faithfulness, gentleness and self-control. Against such things there is no law,"* (Galatians 5:22-23; emphasis added), these are just a few.

For quite some time now I have been trying to come up with a way to collect all the Bible says about Spiritual Maturity and its many characteristics and put it into a format that would be easy to remember and simple to apply in order to wrap our minds around what it means to be like Christ.

Do you remember the t-shirts and bracelets WWJD? It was a great idea, a way to help bring to mind that we are supposed to be like Christ. The one problem though is, too many people don't know who Jesus really was, let alone what He would do.

Once during a marriage counseling session I read Ephesians 5 to a young couple. I explained that marriage is to a representation of our relationship with Christ. I encouraged her to be respectful to him and that he needed to love her the way Christ loves us. I learned later that on the drive home he told his wife that Christ had laid down a lot of rules and expectations so in the same way, it was not only his right, but that by doing the same, he would be doing what Jesus did.

I have found most churches have a mission statement which addresses discipleship, usually something along the line of "disciples who make disciples." A few outstanding churches have even come up with a discipleship process; steps or components in order to get someone on the road toward achieving spiritual growth. But the majority has left it alone hoping it will just happen in time through the knowledge gained in church and/or small groups, but without any real indicators of what it is to become mature and complete.

The Barna Group also found in their spiritual maturity study that: *"Most pastors' struggle with feeling the relevance as well as articulating a specific set of objectives for spirituality, often favoring activities over attitudes"* (emphasis added).

The research among pastors highlighted several inter-related challenges. First, while nearly nine out of 10 pastors said that a lack of spiritual maturity is the most significant or one of the largest problems facing the nation, a minority of pastors believe that spiritual immaturity is a problem in their church. A second challenge is that only a minority of churches has a written statement expressing the outcomes they are looking for in spiritually mature people. A third challenge is that pastors often favor activities over perspectives in their definitions of spiritual maturity. Their metrics for people's spirituality include the practice of spiritual disciplines (19%), involvement in church activities (15%), witnessing to others (15%), having a relationship with Jesus (14%), having concern for others (14%), applying the Bible to life (12%), being willing to grow spiritually (12%), and having knowledge of Scripture (9%).[15]

My goal in writing this book was to come up with a way to measure and understand spiritual maturity so a person may gain victory in their life and to live life as an example of what God can do through Christ and the power of the Holy Spirit in a victorious, healthy, and mature believer.

I have been praying and seeking God for wisdom in what it takes to become spiritually mature, as well as asking godly men how they would measure spiritual development. Through these discussions and my own study of Scripture, I have found there are five areas that come up time and time again. Many of the individual characteristics of a mature believer fall into more than one of these five areas, but the overarching areas in which a healthy believer needs to develop in are:

1. Biblical Wisdom
2. Growing Faith
3. Balanced Priorities
4. Godly Character
5. Sacrificial Service

At this point these areas are just words which might mean something different to everyone who reads them, so my intent through these next chapters is to clarify what they mean, as well as give some Biblical examples for each one. This book is not a study of spiritual maturity, but rather it is to act as a measuring rod in your journey toward Spiritual growth. The goal is for you to experience God at a greater level in each of these areas of your life, and to become healthy, receiving the blessings that come with it. Throughout your life you will be able to come back to these five areas and measure your progress. Only remember without the Holy Spirit leading and empowering you no real change will take place.

As with any personal discipline, there are two offenders to beware of; pride and defeat. Defeat will come if you are pursuing victorious life change in your own strength. You cannot make this happen in your life. Even so there will be times you struggle. "Watch and pray so that you will not fall into temptation. The spirit is willing, but the flesh is weak" (Mark 14:38). "For though the righteous fall seven times, they rise again" (Proverbs 24:16). You will fall, but don't dwell on your failures, continue to seek God, he will reward you.

The scarier offender is pride. It sneaks its way in and can devastate all in its path. God will not stand for it or tolerate it. If you think you have got it all together, be careful, because there is nothing you have gained which God has not given you. God will humble you if you do not humble yourself. The presence of pride in a person's life is a deep seeded issue of spiritual immaturity, of which most are often totally unaware. Pray hard God would reveal any pride holding you back from what He desires in your life.

PART 2:

BIBLICAL WISDOM

Chapter 6

SCHOOL OF HARD KNOCKS
◎

The beginning of wisdom is this: Get wisdom. Though it cost all you have, get understanding. Proverbs 4:7

"Who is wise and understanding among you? Let him show it by his good life, by deeds done in the humility that comes from wisdom" (James 3:13). A while back my wife, Sacha bought folders from Staples, but once she got home she realized they had only charged her for three, not seven. When she returned to the store the cashier became flustered.

Sacha asked her, "What's the problem?"

She replied, "Well, no one has ever come back before to pay for something, so I don't know how to complete this transaction".

My wife proceeded to gently explain to the woman all she needed to do was to ring up the additional folders. Her inability to solve the problem was painful enough, preceded only by the sad fact that my wife was the first person the cashier had ever experienced coming back.

Our life is a series of choices: how we act on the road, cutting people off or speeding; how we manage our finances, how we react to what life throws at us. The sum of all your choices spells out your life. Major or small, all of them boil down to your wisdom.

I was a youth pastor for ten years, and well, youth pastors aren't really known for wisdom. If we can pull off something stupid to get a laugh from kids, then we'll do it, praying all along we survive through it. One time our youth group back-packed up a mountain. After we set up our tents there wasn't much to do, since we weren't at a lake. I decided some entertainment was in order. There was a great hill to roll down. Before long, the youth had taken a few controlled rolls down the hill. I thought,

"I know what would be fun; I should pretend to spin out of control a little as I go down, it would look hilarious."

Hilarious is indeed what happened, as my pretending turned into reality and I plummeted down the hill completely out of control, right into the trees and bushes which eventually stopped my fall. As I staggered back up the hill with my shirt and pants completely shredded I was so thankful that God chose to protect me in the midst of my stupidity so my kids didn't have to pack me out with a broken leg.

Very rarely does great understanding come over night. There is a reason why we attribute wisdom to the elderly. Often they have put in the time to gain knowledge and they have seen it lived out in many different ways, with different results. This is often referred to as, "the school of hard knocks." For many of us we tend to live life like this, going through life experiencing things as they come, hopefully coming out on the other side a little bit wiser. I don't know about you, but no thanks. There are too many things that are too important to mess up, and all too often becoming wiser on the other side is too little, too late. Besides, who wants to go through that kind of pain? Lost jobs, hurt feelings, broken families, wayward children, financial strain, depression, addictions; to name a few.

Yes, pain can be a great teacher, but only if you care to learn and usually it only gives you understanding on how not to do something, not necessarily how to do it right. The saddest thing is there are too many things we only get to do once. No, I would rather gain wisdom now.

Many of you, like me, do long for wisdom now, while we're in the thick of it. We come to a place where the lack of wisdom has produced some trial or pain and so we call out, "God give me wisdom in what to do!" He can and He will, but sometimes due to our unwillingness to seek, He allows pain to be our teacher. Psalms 119:71 reads, "It was good for me to be afflicted so that I might learn your decrees;" Proverbs 22:3 says, "The prudent see danger and take refuge, but the simple keep going and pay the penalty."

Parenting is an incredible journey no one can properly prepare you for. My wife and I worked hard to prepare our girls for when they grew up, by allowing them more and more decision making throughout their high school years. But we were still caught unawares at how much of a shock it was for them once they graduated. We have three at college right now, watching them try to decide what courses to take, where they should live, work, and then, should they even be at college? It's been overwhelming for them, and it has been an interesting challenge for us to give advice when asked and to learn to be quiet when not asked. As we let them grow up we have to let them make mistakes as well.

Life is full of choices and therefore full of danger. I desire to make wise choices and live a life of good, not pain of my own making. The basics of wisdom are: the fear of God, an understanding granted by the Holy Spirit, and a life lived in obedience to God. This kind of wisdom, Biblical wisdom, is mentioned over and over in Proverbs; with a continual reminder of the good that comes from it and the pain that comes to those who don't have it.

Throughout Scripture instructions are handed down from father and mother to their young children. They believed the young could be wise if they desire. So, what about you? Do you really desire to be wise?

"Blessed are those whose ways are blameless, who walk according to the law of the LORD. Blessed are those who keep his statutes and seek him with all their heart—they do no wrong but follow his ways. You have laid down precepts that are to be fully obeyed" (Psalms 119:1—4).

If wisdom is rooted in understanding God, shown by obedience and granted through the power of the Holy Spirit, what is our part? It is to desire and seek it. There is no greater way to gain Biblical wisdom than to be in the Bible itself. What better way is there to have an understanding of who God is than to read his Word? How can you be obedient if you do not know His teachings? Why would the Holy Spirit give you what you do not seek? "I seek you with all my heart; do not let me stray from your commands" (Psalm 119:10).

Target Practice

I would like to help you understand how much you look to God on a daily basis and hopefully increase your desire to seek Him more. If you are reading this book to gain greater understanding of your life with Christ, I would venture to say that you do seek and wish for the presence of God in your life. The problem for most of us is we just get too busy and before we know it the day has come and gone.

So here is the challenge. Set your watch or phone to beep once every sixty minutes, and when you hear the beep take just a minute to thank the Lord or praise Him. Do this for a week. It's not hard, but I think you will enjoy the outcome. If that is too easy try every thirty minutes. Try not to make it a request time, but rather a time to acknowledge Him and praise Him.

Chapter 7

THE IMPOSTER
◎

Jesus replied, "Are you not in error because you do not know the Scriptures or the power of God?
Mark 12:24

B iblical Wisdom is different from Biblical knowledge. Wisdom is linked to knowledge and is dependent upon it to grow, but knowledge does not necessarily give way to wisdom.

For years now, American society has pursued knowledge as though it were the key to all things. We pressure our children toward higher education only to leave them drowning in debt caused by school loans, making it nearly impossible for them to make wise financial decisions as they begin their adult life. I'm not saying higher education does not have its place, but what I am saying is that many of these college students have no idea what courses to pursue, so they are without a compass—drowning in debt because they feel pressured to fulfill society's expectations of them.

The pursuit of knowledge is a self discipline that can benefit the seeker, but the truth of the matter is only what is applied to life has any real benefit. Our society gives great admiration to those who are educated; placing higher value on those who have a title before their name. We love to sit under those who will give us more knowledge to add to our learning.

The pursuit of knowledge can be beneficial, but in and of itself it does not lead to wisdom and yet so often we attribute spiritual maturity to those who know more than we do.

The idea that great knowledge exhibits spiritual maturity is humanistic in nature. It is not godly. 1 Corinthians 8:1 says, "But knowledge puffs up while love builds up." The pursuit of more information can lead to, and often does lead to pride when it is not coupled with wisdom.

The pursuit of wisdom and understanding is something altogether different. The Pharisees of Christ's time were known for their knowledge of the Scripture, but they had no spiritual understanding. Not only did they have a hard time with Jesus because He did not fit their ideal (knowledge) about who the Christ would be or come from, but these ideals often lead to their being put to shame by uneducated people; like the man born blind[16], or Peter and John in Acts 4:13, "Now when they saw the boldness of Peter and John, and perceived that they were uneducated common men they were astonished." Jesus likened the Pharisees to the blind leading the blind[17], and much of their downfall was a result of their pride. For their knowledge did not align with what was going on spiritually around them.

For example: they believed miracles only came from God, but that godly men wouldn't dare break the rules of righteous living they had prescribed, to heal someone. Jesus was not a sinner by God's standard, but He was according to theirs. They were unable to humble themselves and look at it differently. Their knowledge earned them a place of authority, a title before their name, yet Christ warned that their knowledge held them back from true wisdom. As a matter of fact Christ's wisdom was foolishness to them. I wish we could say this kind of pride does not exist today but, it is alive and well.

When we started our church in Montana we asked ourselves,

"Why are the un-churched in Montana not in church, what holds them back?"

We realized most people live in Montana for the great outdoors; to ask them to give up every weekend to be a part of something they had never experienced before was too much. Their weekends were what they lived for, so we decided to do church mid-week. I had no idea how much the tradition of a Sunday services was ingrained into people. The idea of a mid-week service is extremely offensive to many good church people. Many believe we have sold out in order to bring people to church, others believe we shouldn't even be considered a real church. The truth of the matter is we probably would have more people in our building if we met on Sunday but they would be church people. It is the sick who need a doctor, so they are who we will go to; even if many of my peers think I'm the sick one.

The church must be careful because we are on the same road as the Pharisees, headed toward our own downfall. Just look around at all the books, Bible studies, and great teachers we have; yet the influence the church is making on this country is greatly lacking. Many times we limit those who can minister to the ones with all the right degrees and higher learning. This leads the masses to believe they are not adequate to do the work of God, because they lack the knowledge.

This is not Christ's plan. Look at those He chose. "Brothers and sisters, think of what you were when you were called. Not many of you were wise by human standards; not many were influential; not many were of noble birth. But God chose the foolish things of the world to shame the wise; God chose the weak things of the world to shame the strong" (1 Corinthians 1:26-27).

Not to mention verses like 1 John 2:27, "As for you, the anointing you received from him remains in you, and you do not need anyone to teach you. But as his anointing teaches you about all things and as that anointing is real, not counterfeit—just as it has taught you, remain in him." If your first reaction is to run to a community to have someone explain this verse better to you, you have the problem I am talking about. It is not wrong to want understanding, but we should first and foremost turn to the Lord and ask the Holy Spirit to show us the meaning. To think it must come from someone else diminishes the power of the Holy Spirit. I'm not saying there is no value in Godly counsel, but do not underestimate the power of the Holy Spirit speaking into your life in a way no man can.

One of the men I meet with on a weekly basis to talk about what we are reading in Scripture has a heart for the hurting and down and out. He puts a lot of time into serving others. As he read the passage about Mary anointing Jesus' feet, the phrase, "you will always have the poor with you," [18] hit him hard. As he prayed about it, his wife said something about all she had on her plate. In that moment, the Spirit spoke to him and he realized—there will always be good things to do but the most important thing was to be at Jesus' feet, not chasing after the constant needs of everything else. God spoke to him in a way he needed to hear. I would have given him some other bit of insight, something biblical I believe, but it would not have brought about the life change only the Spirit of God can.

Target Practice

It surprises me how many believers have not heard the Holy Spirit speak to them. It is a supernatural thing but it should not be a rare thing. If you have not felt the Holy Spirit speaking to you, maybe it is because you are looking for a burning bush or writing on the wall. The truth is the Spirit speaks through many ways; through the Bible as He brings understanding, through the use of others to speak to you (hopefully you have experienced this through a sermon), but sometimes it could simply be someone walking by. Some refer to it as the still, small voice inside of you. This voice is more than just your conscience. I have experienced the Holy Spirit speak to me in ways that could only be God; from thoughts out of context, to being awakened at night with an idea that is filled with peace or urgency, to insights that were given I had no prior knowledge of.

The Spirit desires to speak to you, but are you ready to listen? If God says something, you best do it. If you are ready to follow Christ in this way, start praying that God would speak to you, and when something comes to mind, act on it and see what happens. The more you do, the more you will hear from the Spirit.

Chapter 8

APPLYING UNDERSTANDING
◎

When they saw the courage of Peter and John and realized that they were unschooled, ordinary men, they were astonished and they took note that these men had been with Jesus. Acts 4:13

Acts 4:5-20 is an example of common, uneducated men filled with the Holy Spirit showing great wisdom. Their knowledge of Christ coupled with the Fear of God— this is Biblical wisdom. There are other forms of wisdom out there. For instance, common sense is a form of wisdom. It is an understanding of how things work in nature or in people and knowing how to act accordingly. Some people have a lot of business sense. They understand the ins and outs of the business world. I like to think I have a good understanding of nature. As a kid I spent most of my time chasing things through the woods, hunting, fishing and camping. In high school I even skipped an entire semester just to trap for the winter season. I have no idea why the school allowed it; perhaps they were just glad to get rid of me. Some of the boys at the school my girls attend liked to call me the mountain man, since I love to live off the land, providing for my family while exploring the great outdoors. Since I have all daughters I have done nothing to correct their overestimation of me.

The Bible also talks about the wisdom of this age, which is basically an understanding of the popular beliefs of the time. This is worldly wisdom. Having knowledge or understanding in these areas is not a bad thing, unless it is contrary to Biblical wisdom. In fact, it would do us all good if there was more common sense in people. But common sense, business sense, even "being a mountain man", is not Biblical wisdom.

Biblical wisdom is true wisdom. It does not change over time like all other forms of wisdom. Biblical wisdom is rooted in the understanding of God, "who does not change like shifting shadows" (James 1:17b).

I have been using the word understanding, because having knowledge of something is different than understanding it, in my opinion. Knowing something or the gaining of knowledge is the gathering of information and facts about something. Understanding, as I am using it, is allowing information and facts to influence your thinking and actions; it becomes part of you.

(Knowledge + understanding) x application = wisdom

How wise you are is greatly determined by how you apply what you know and understand. In other words your knowledge and understanding may not be that great, but if you are applying all you are learning, then you can have the same or even much greater wisdom than someone with little application but great knowledge.

I was raised in construction, my dad and all three of my brothers have been contractors. So, construction has come pretty easy to me; working on cars has never been my thing. One day my truck needed new brake pads, so I decided to try my hand at fixing my own brakes. I went over to my neighbor's home and asked him to give me step by step directions on how to change the brakes. I was pretty pleased with myself, that I had done it right and conquered something mechanically. All I needed was for my wife to come and pump the brakes. I asked Sacha to pump the brakes while I worked on them from below. She started pumping, but the brakes still didn't work. She pumped and pumped some more, still no brakes. I dragged myself back to the neighbors and reviewed the steps and according to him I'd done everything right. I called my wife and asked her to pump the brakes again, while I lay down in front of the truck tires to see what the problem was. Suddenly the truck lunged at me, as my life flashed before my eyes; I realized exactly what the problem was. I leapt up with an incredulous look on my face and yelled,

"Sacha, were you pumping the clutch the whole time?"

Ah, yes she indeed had been pumping the clutch the whole time. The funny thing about this story is Sacha has driven a stick for a long time. She has great knowledge of the difference between the clutch, brake and accelerator. She has driven a stick since she was seventeen years old, so the problem wasn't her understanding. In her words, the problem was her blonde hair. But the real problem lay in the fact that she had knowledge and understanding, but her application was way off.

Biblical wisdom is learning or gaining the knowledge of God and the Bible, and allowing it to change and influence the way we act and think. One way our Biblical wisdom is demonstrated is in how we treat others. The Bible has given us an understanding of God's grace, which in turn should change the way we give grace to others. Someone who can't stand other people, or is mad or upset or prejudice because of another person's age, gender, race, political stance, or sin does not *understand* the gospel of Christ although they may *know* the gospel.

I know a few people who have an abundance of knowledge, but no wisdom. James 2:19-20 refers to demons in a similar manner, "You believe that there is one God. Good! Even the demons believe that—and shudder. You foolish person, do you want evidence that faith without deeds is useless?" The pursuit of more knowledge will not bring wisdom. I would go so far as to say there are some who need to repent from their pursuit of knowledge because they have not acted on or chosen to understand it.

"Do not merely listen to the word, and so deceive yourselves. Do what it says. Anyone who listens to the word but does not do what it says is like someone who looks at his face in a mirror and, after looking at himself, goes away and immediately forgets what he looks like. But whoever looks intently into the perfect law that gives freedom, and continues in it—not forgetting what they have heard, but doing it—they will be blessed in what they do" (James 1:22—25).

Wisdom is proven in actions. As Forest Gump's mother would say, "Stupid is as stupid does."[19] And so, wisdom is proven by her actions.

Target Practice

The proof of Biblical wisdom is your life choices. Really every choice you make; what you do and don't do, the things you entertain yourself with, with whom and where you take a drink or two, how often you spend your money and whether you have the money at the time, to what extent you justify your actions and choices, how you find comfort and whether it has control over you. Whether it is work, play, eating, the internet, spending money, etc.; any choice you make shows your Biblical wisdom. Many of these choices are not sin or bad in and of themselves, but what do your choices say about you and where do they lead? A wise man anticipates the path ahead.

Look back through all the choices you have made from the first choice you can remember, to the ones you've made this morning. These are a reflection of your wisdom. Sure there are things that are out of your control but what put you there and what did you do with your circumstances? The majority of regret, pain and sorrow we face come from the choices we make in accordance with our wisdom. It is important to note however, there will be times we experience pain because of wise choices we've made, such as when you decide to live in integrity and your boss or friend is asking you to look the other way. Even though you will experience pain in doing what is right, you will live without regret, for your character has stood the test.

Chapter 9

FEAR OF THE LORD
◎

The fear of the LORD is the beginning of knowledge,
but fools despise wisdom and instruction. Proverbs 1:7

Proverbs is full of wisdom. It seems like every other verse is talking directly about wisdom. Showing the benefit it will bring to your life, and the warning for those who lack it. Proverbs points out that the righteous are wise, and wisdom is to be desired above all other pursuits in life. I have mentioned knowledge doesn't give way to wisdom, but it can be harmful as well, if not joined to wisdom. So how do we grow in wisdom, or where to we even start?

Proverbs 1:7 reads, "The fear of the Lord is the beginning of wisdom". Now this is not very popular in today's sermons or teachings. We would much rather sing about being a friend of God, or how merciful He is. But the truth of the matter is His mercy and friendship is only experienced in light of our fear of Him. Fear is something that we feel uncomfortable with as Christians. We tend to avoid these verses. Others argue the word doesn't mean fear, but rather loving reverence. True reverence does not exist without some fear.

"Do not be wise in your own eyes; fear the LORD and shun evil" (Proverbs 3:7). I do not think I need to explain in too much detail why we should fear a supernatural being who has spoken the universe into existence; has created you, knows you down to the number of hairs on your head, and is so holy He will not allow the slightest sin to remain un-dealt with. There are some attributes of God which put us in a very unpleasant place, and it is easy to dismiss them for more comfortable ones, but this is not wise.

A couple of years ago my good friend David and I went on an elk hunt together. It was his first elk hunt and we would be backpacking in five miles to set up camp. It had rained the night before so we had a few puddles to step over as we hiked up. But there was something wrong with the puddles, they were too uniformed in size and the spacing between was even. With closer observation we realized they were huge grizzly tracks; bigger than I'd ever come across in my lifetime. It put us on guard, which was not a bad thing, as just another mile down the trail we jumped two black bear cubs on the trail. Black bears are really not a big deal, but cubs and a mother can be bad news. We stood still till they left and never did see the mom. But the grizzly tracks, which are very different from a black bear's, were still headed up the trail. The bear had walked about five miles and disappeared about a quarter of a mile from where we set up camp. We took some extra precautions that night, but I had hunted around grizzly before so I was not overly concerned. In the middle of the night we heard elk bugling and as daybreak came I knew right where they were. About two hours later I shot a big bull elk with my bow. , and so begun the hard work of butchering and packing out an 800 pound elk. David helped, but the next day I sent him off to hunt while I made the last trips of meat to the truck.

That night I came in to camp just before dusk, exhausted, smelling like elk blood and sweat. I just wanted to clean up and go to bed. Just as I was getting the water hot David showed up looking rather unhinged. As darkness fell He told me how he had gotten into elk, but could not close the deal. On the way back to camp he had seen the grizzly tracks again and had heard a lot of noise down in the creek bottom. He skirted around the area, but he thought he could hear something following him to camp; now I knew why he looked so unhinged. It ran through my mind that if you startle a grizzly there is a good chance they will leave you alone, but if a grizzly hunts you, there is not much hope. Right then we heard a loud snap, as a branch broke about one-hundred yard from where David had just come from. We quickly grabbed our bear spray and yelled out "Hey bear, Hey bear" in the hopes of scaring it. Suddenly we could hear something running through the trees breaking branches and heading straight towards us, we had scared it all right; the only problem was we scared it right into our camp! We jumped behind a tree and screamed like little girls until it was over. Fear was the only thing running through my blood at that time. The animal barreled through within twenty feet of our camp; ran right past us and kept going. We did not sleep at all that night. The morning light revealed it was two moose that had run through the camp; we had a good laugh at each other and breathed a little easier. I still don't like the fact that Dave knows I can scream like a girl.

Fear is a powerful emotion. It has the tendency to change the way we do things. Because of the fear we felt that night there are a few things I do differently when camping in grizzly country. Fear will stop us from getting onto a boat if we fear the water or a plane if we fear heights. When we are put in a place we fear, like a child in a dark room, we cannot focus on anything but our fear. Fear changes the way we do things. Apply this to the fear of God. If we fear God, we think twice before doing something that would not please Him, and begin to look for ways to please Him. "It is a fearful thing to fall into the hands of the living God" (Hebrews 10:31). As Christians I think we've lost some of that. Do I really walk in fear of God? Do I understand who I stand before and pray to? Does it take root in my heart that he is a holy and mighty God?

Even though I live in Montana, I don't drive ninety miles an hour, because I fear the law. It would be fun to drive fast, but I also fear the increase in my insurance. Fear stops us from doing things, but it only motivates us through punishment or loss. If you live in fear of somebody you will stop doing things because you fear them, but it won't motivate you beyond the fear you have for them.

Target Practice

What is your understanding of God, of Christ? The way you look at Him, your understanding of His character and how He works, His authority, and your personal interactions with Him will lay the ground work for a proper fear of, or for some, a misguided fear of God. This is the place to start praying for wisdom. Spend some time right now doing just that. As for the future, begin every time you read the Bible, listen to a spiritual conversation or sermon, with prayer that the Holy Spirit would give you wisdom in what you are hearing.

Chapter 10

PROPER MOTIVATION
◎

There is no fear in love. But perfect love drives out
fear, because fear has to do with punishment. The one
who fears is not made perfect in love. 1 John 4:18

W hat truly motivates us? Love does. Love compels
us to do something. I am in love with my wife and
there are a lot of things I do, not for my benefit or pleasure,
but because they please her. When children feel secure in
their family their love compels them to help and serve.

I remember one day when Sacha was working hard at
cleaning the windows, which is no small task with three preschoolers under foot. She started in the dining and living
rooms where the girls watched her in awe, she then worked
her way through the bedrooms. She was thrilled that she actually managed to complete the task, since the kids were obviously playing quietly and left her undisturbed to get it done.

But then as we walked back into the living room, her heart sank as she heard the girls say with big grins on their faces,

"Look mommy, we help."

Yeah, they helped all right. Wet toilet paper was stuck all over the windows as they scrubbed hard to serve just like their Mommy. Where they got the wet toilet paper is still a mystery we never want to solve.

"The only thing that counts is faith expressing itself through love" (Galatians 5:6). When our children were young, they knew we loved them more than anyone; when they got hurt they would run to us, they gave us kisses, dandelions, they drew pictures for us with their crayons, and they would cry when we were gone from them. However, there were certain naughty things they would do that love did not stop. When we were gone they would take those same crayons and draw on the walls. Love did not stop them from doing it again, but the fear of our discipline sure did. Fear changed their behavior and in turn, it made them wiser. Do they draw on the walls out of love? No, it's their heart's desire. What stops them the next time is fear. Fear and love together.

You have seen families who are all love and no discipline. Their kids lack fear and total chaos ensues. I have also seen families ruled and controlled by fear, where their kids are doormats and slaves, terrified to say anything or to step out of line.

You might be thinking that I'm not talking about wisdom but obedience. But I believe obedience is the proof of wisdom. In Luke 1:17, John the Baptist is described as preparing the way for Christ by bringing the disobedient to a place of repentance, or the recognition of wrong and the turning away from it, which is said to be the wisdom of the righteous. Repentance is the birth place of spiritual maturity.

Therefore, wisdom is obedience, coupled with understanding. And so increased understanding should lead to increased obedience. This is where we need help, for we all start out blind to who God is. "And even if our gospel is veiled, it is veiled to those who are perishing. The god of this age has blinded the minds of unbelievers, so that they cannot see the light of the gospel that displays the glory of Christ, who is the image of God" (2 Corinthians 4:3-4).

Without an understanding of God or Christ, there can be no fear of God or love for that matter. We need someone to shed light on the subject in order for our understanding to begin. "For God, who said, 'Let light shine out of darkness,' made his light shine in our hearts to give us the light of the knowledge of God's glory displayed in the face of Christ"(2 Corinthians 4:6). Note how this talks about the glory of God which is fearful for a sinner and the face of Christ which is the hope of incredible love. Moreover, I want you to see, it is God who gives us the light of knowledge. James 1:5 says it this way, "If any of you lacks wisdom, you should ask God, who gives generously to all without finding fault, and it will be given to you."

Asking God to give you wisdom is the second key. It is only through the Holy Spirit that we are given the understanding of our knowledge. There are those who have read the whole Bible through and have found nothing of great importance to themselves, and there are countless others who have only heard a handful of verses who have experienced complete life change. In my experience, regardless of how good or bad a sermon is delivered unless the Holy Spirit brings understanding, it will not result in lifelong change.

Part of asking God to give us wisdom has to do with our desire to gain wisdom. God's desire is for us to desire him. This is evident in the work of salvation. There is no salvation for someone who does not desire God.

> For although they knew God, they neither glorified him as God nor gave thanks to him, but their thinking became futile and their foolish hearts were darkened. Although they claimed to be wise, they became fools and exchanged the glory of the immortal God for images made to look like a mortal human being and birds and animals and reptiles. Therefore God gave them over in the sinful desires of their hearts, to sexual impurity for the degrading of their bodies with one another (Romans 1:21—24a).

We see that a desire for God is the key to pleasing God. "And without faith it is impossible to please God, because anyone who comes to Him must believe that He exists and that He rewards those who earnestly seek Him" (Hebrews 11:6). To earnestly seek Him is probably the most important part of all our prayers. Too many times to note here, He tells us that He will answer our prayers. We will talk about prayer later, but for now, take note, a desire for God is of great importance when it comes to seeing our prayers answered. When it comes to seeing prayers answered and seeing wisdom granted, you must know it is the work of the Holy Spirit.

Target Practice

S.O.A.P.

Scripture: Start by dedicating time to read your Bible. Set aside some time everyday to S.O.A.P. It doesn't have to be long and you don't need to set a goal of how much to read. Remember, it is about understanding, not knowledge.

Observation: If you do not stop and think about it, what is the point? Ask what is it talking about or to whom is it talking to? Ask yourself what stands out to you, and is there something new you have not noticed before. Anticipate the Holy Spirit speaking to you about what you are reading, but you must slow down and listen. I would challenge you to write down what you are learning or what is confusing to you.

Application: How does what you have learned change your thinking or what do you need to do with it? This might be the hardest part, but this is where wisdom takes hold or not.

Pray: Remember prayer should be a part of everything. Asking God to show you what He wants you to know or do. Just talk to him about what you have read and ask for wisdom to carry it out.

PART 3:

GROWING FAITH

Chapter 11

FAITH LIKE A MUSTARD SEED
◎

"If you remain in me and my words remain in you, ask whatever you wish, and it will be given you" (John 15:7).

Often people talk about faith as if it were the major ingredient to a blessed life.

"If only you had enough faith then..."

They believe the measure of their faith controls what does or does not happen in their life. This is faith in faith, the idea that you can get God to do anything for you if you just believe hard enough for it. You see this concept is repeated often in the prosperity doctrine, which is the teaching that if you are on God's side He will make you rich, and when He doesn't it is because you are either full of sin or you just don't have enough faith.

When my youngest was a year old she contracted fifth disease; a common childhood illness like chicken pox. Unfortunately my wife also got ill and suffered rare complications to the virus, which lead to her being bedridden for six months, followed by another eighteen months of light activity with chronic joint pain and fatigue. To say these times were rough doesn't even begin to describe what we went through. Our three girls were all under five years old at the start of her illness. I was in the middle of building a three story youth center and couldn't stop the project. It was a tremendously painful season, as my wife parented from a LAZ-Y boy. During this time we received a lot of prayer and many well-meaning Christians told my wife she just needed more faith. Sacha wrestled with this over and over again. Was it really that she didn't have faith? She had seen her mother healed from arthritis, she had prayed and others had been healed, so was her faith lacking?

I think there is a common misunderstanding of the connection between faith and the trials we suffer. The fact that someone is continuing to endure through something truly horrific really has nothing to do with their lack of faith. I would say it would be quite the opposite. I believe their ability to withstand such pain and to continue to hold fast to the understanding of a loving God in the midst of it takes great faith.

In Acts 3 it describes a man who had been lame from birth. Scripture says he was carried and laid daily at the gate of the temple to ask for alms. When Jesus came he healed multitudes of people, but this man was not healed. Imagine his pain, his suffering, knowing that Jesus was healing the lame, the blind, the demon possessed, but he was not healed. God in his perfect timing delayed his healing until he begged Peter and John for money; God is never late. God's delay accomplished a purpose beyond our understanding and in his perfect timing to bring Him glory.

Your circumstances have little to do with the amount or lack of your faith. It is our reactions to our circumstances that reveal our faith. To believe God is going to do something in the future is not wrong and it is faith, but it is an incomplete measure of a person's faith. I believe a more accurate measure of faith is the peace a person has that God is working regardless of the outcome. What I'm getting at is, not only do we misunderstand faith sometimes, but our misunderstanding is commonly how we measure faith. The things we feel we were a part of that God has done and whether we believed He could or would do it before hand is the measuring rod we tend to use to measure our faith, but this can lead to a faulty conclusion.

Our faith begins like a mustard seed when we first believe. Without this "mustard seed" there is no pleasing God, but this is just the beginning. Faith does grow and mature, but it grows in proportion to our understanding of God and our journey with Him. You see true faith is not based on us, but rather on the works and attributes of the trinity.

The more a person begins to understand God's sovereignty, power, and love, for those who are His, the more our heart proclaims with Paul,

"No, in all these things we are more than conquerors through him who loved us. For I am convinced that neither death nor life, neither angels nor demons, neither the present nor the future, nor any powers, neither height nor depth, nor anything else in all creation, will be able to separate us from the love of God that is in Christ Jesus our Lord" (Romans 8:37—39).

Romans 8:31 reads, "What, then, shall we say in response to these things? If God is for us, who can be against us?"

You see, our problem is not in believing God *will* do something, but that He *is* doing, and is in all things that happen, even the pain and suffering is for His purpose and for our good if we will trust Him. "And we know that in all things God works for the good of those who love him, who have been called according to his purpose" (Romans 8:28).

Target practice

Our battle lies in the simple fact that we see only the circumstances of our surroundings. The victory comes when we can look to eternal things, knowing that our circumstances will change.

Make a list of what you are wrestling with. On one side write what falls under circumstances and on the other side what is happening that is eternal. The list might just surprise you.

"Therefore we do not lose heart. Though outwardly we are wasting away, yet inwardly we are being renewed day by day. For our light and momentary troubles are achieving for us an eternal glory that far outweighs them all. So we fix our eyes not on what is seen, but on what is unseen, since what is seen is temporary, but what is unseen is eternal" (2 Corinthians 4:16—18).

Now pray for peace over your temporary circumstances, that you may stand through His power. Also, pray you will fix your eyes on what is eternal.

Chapter 12

WHEN HARD TIMES COME
◎

*Consider it pure joy, my brothers and sisters, when-
ever you face trials of many kinds, because you
know that the testing of your faith produces perseverance. Let perseverance finish its work so that you
may be mature and complete, not lacking anything.*
James 1:2-4

I believe this is why God allows various trials to come into
our life, "These have come so that the proven genuineness
of your faith—of greater worth than gold, which perishes
even though refined by fire—may result in praise, glory and
honor when Jesus Christ is revealed" (1 Peter 1:7). It is a
testing, not of whether we have faith, but rather a strengthening of our faith as we go through more than we have before.

Let's face it, when everything is going good, we often fall
into a state of mind that we are OK. We don't need anything

from God. We have a sense that we are in control. Often it is not until we lose control or when things are beyond our control that we cry out for God. Many people confess it is during a crisis or trial that they feel closest to God. Not surprisingly those who find themselves relying on God for a prolonged time tend to grow in their faith. Even to a place where they not only find comfort through the trial, but come to a place of peace regardless of the outcome.

When our church began we met on our property in a poly shelter building; commonly used for hay storage. Eventually as our church grew, we added more shelters to accommodate the different classes for children's church. One day we heard about google earth and ran to our computer to find out what our home looked like from the sky. Slowly the picture emerged and we sat in stunned silence of the view of our 'compound' in the heart of the Montanan mountains. We finally realized why the UPS guy acted so nervous every time he delivered a package!

One winter we had a terrible snowstorm and our main sanctuary collapsed. It was a crushing blow to realize we had nowhere to meet. As we shoveled out the snow we discovered even though the tent was a total loss, everything else was fine; the video projector, sound board, every chair and table was safe. As we processed purchasing a new shelter we realized that maybe God was helping us to move out of our comfortable nest.

At the same time a member of our church lost his business. His brand new 6000 square foot warehouse building was being emptied that week. We could see God moving even though we knew this was a huge financial step for our church. And so, the incredible faith journey began as we trusted in Him to provide for us to insulate and remodel the building for the church.

To be honest, during that time it actually wasn't that hard to have faith. Our circumstances were so beyond us we knew only a miracle would help our church survive. I often have found it is harder to have faith in the little things; the ongoing trials and frustrations in our life, especially when we come to a crossroads and have to pray through the options before us.

I believe the amount of peace a person has in their life shows how much faith they have in the sovereignty and love of God. Jesus alludes to this place of faith when he talks about anxiety in Matthew 5. Now it is one thing to say "do not be anxious about..." and it is another to put those needs or thoughts to rest and trust in God.

When Sacha and I met we spoke of our passion to invest in youth in a rural setting. After completing a youth internship we were ready for the next step in our adventure of serving Christ. We prayed and prayed, were interviewed and finally felt a specific calling to a small logging community in the heart of the mountains in Eastern Washington. We were nervous wanting to know if God was truly calling us to this community. The only solution was to lay a Washington state map on the ground, turn our backs and toss a coin over our shoulder. And in case you are wondering, if God can put a coin in the mouth of a fishes, he can certainly land a coin on the town of Republic! Looking back now, I just shake my head. But we were in love; we had a passion and a heart for people and were ready to serve God. We loaded all we had in a trailer and off we went. We had no job, nowhere to live, but we knew we were called. People back then talked of our great faith. But believe me, to load up your new wife and a small trailer with your worldly possessions does not take great faith. We had nothing to lose and everything to gain.

Ten years later to load up my family of five, with a whole lot more than a small little trailer; leaving a life with regular support, a healthy ministry and a three story youth center to follow God's call to church planting in Montana was a true test of faith. Yes, we had lived on faith support for thirteen years, but God had blessed us with valuable, consistent givers we were able to count on for steady, monthly support. That was not the case for us with church planting. We literally began without any support, praying for God to provide. He has faithfully continued to provide, although not necessarily in the timing we would have desired. For most of our years of church planting our grocery shopping list was our prayer list and more than once we not only did not get paid, but personally carried the church bills as well.

When our family has hurt the most financially, we took a step back and remembered God's faithful provision.

Even as newlyweds, times were tough. I had started an internship and we literally didn't have a penny to our name. Sacha picked up the mail and sure enough it was all bills. The electric company, gas, phone, insurance, even Day-timers got into the action. My wife was troubled as she opened the first bill, but surprisingly the first bill was a check, and then the next and the next. Seven checks later, we actually had a savings account.

In order to find victory through the trials in your life and to grow your confidence in Him, we must look to God's provision in the past. This isn't really my idea but God's. When the Israelites came out of slavery and were placed into a land to govern themselves, He told the people to tell the story of how He rescued them; provided for them, preformed miracles in their presence and even protected them in the mist of overwhelming ordeals. The Israelites were to tell this story over and over; to even celebrate what He had done for them as a Holy holiday. This was important in helping them to grow in their faith, which reassured them of God's love. "Teach them to your children, talking about them when you sit at home and when you walk along the road, when you lie down and when you get up" (Deuteronomy 11:19).

Target Practice

Try it. Sit down and write out the things that God has done for you in the past. His protection, his provision, the time He has answered your prayers. The other thing I want you to do is to start memorizing verses that are about God's power and love for you. As the Holy Spirit speaks to you about something in your S.O.A.P. take these verses and commit them to memory. It will strengthen your faith and bring you peace.

Chapter 13

WHO ARE YOU PURSUING?
◎

What good is it, my brothers and sisters, if someone claims to have faith but has no deeds? Can such faith save them. James 2:14

This statement about faith and deeds, or works, is a hard one to understand if you hold to the Biblical teaching that we are saved by God's grace alone and not by our work. "For it is by grace you have been saved, through faith—and this is not from yourselves, it is the gift of God— not by works, so that no one can boast" (Ephesians 2:8-9). Not to mention the fact if works, or being good, by obeying God's laws, like the Ten Commandments, can save us then Christ died for no reason. "I do not set aside the grace of God, for if righteousness could be gained through the law, Christ died for nothing!"(Galatians 2:21). No one has ever or will ever be good enough to earn their way to God. As a matter of fact, the law was given to us to show us how impossible it is for us to be good. A simple look at the Ten Commandments reveals we are incapable of fulfilling the law. As a matter of fact, if you have broken one commandment like lying, or wanting what someone else has, you have broken the first 'to have no other gods before me'. You see whatever compelled you to break one of the other laws has become a god to you in the sense of your desire to have or protect it above God's desires of righteousness in you.

As a younger man I have often fought to prove myself through some kind of endeavor. I felt it was important for my identity. One of those passions was hunting. Not that I had to prove to others that I could push beyond my limits, but more to prove it to myself. I remember one elk hunting trip when I hiked into the wilderness by myself and stayed there for sixteen days without seeing a single soul. As an introvert it was awesome. I was proving I was a real and capable man and I loved it. This was incredible for me. The problem was it was not enough. Hunting became my pursuit for meaning and satisfaction. You can only imagine what this was doing to Sacha and my little girls. It even got to the place where hunting no longer provided joy because I pushed myself to the point of believing if I was not successful then maybe I was not a real man. I had taken something God had blessed me with and turned it in to my god. I was paying the price for not pursuing Him.

Anything you believe will provide for you, or bring your life pleasure or meaning, has the potential to become a god.

It is easy to enjoy something to the point of becoming driven to pursue or protect it, which is a form of worship. Look at the workaholic or the alcoholic. Someone who is addicted to something lives their life in pursuit of what they desire. Not only has their desire become a god to them but now they are known by their actions in pursuing their desires. "A tree is recognized by its fruit."[20]

This is in a way what I believe James is saying. If you really have faith in Christ your desire will be for Him, which is seen through your actions. Later James describes a faith that does not change ones actions "You believe that there is one God. Good! Even the demons believe that—and shudder" (James 2:19). This faith is knowledge of something, but it does not produce any action. In James words, this is a dead faith.

So, it is not actions that save us, but the lack of them may point to a lack of true faith. The faith that believes God is the only one who will provide, protect, produce pleasure in and bring meaning to our life will cause us to pursue God as our highest desire, and our actions will reveal this passion; the more intense this belief, the more intense our actions.

Therefore, you can see growing faith is manifested not only by growing peace, but also by growing actions in our life. It is the proof in the pudding. One of the biggest hindrances to this proof is simply we don't truly believe God can or will provide all we need. Or maybe we just want more than we believe He will give us, so we begin our own pursuit of what we desire. We have put our faith in the thing or idea, and trust it to fill us. It has become our master "No one can serve two masters. Either you will hate the one and love the other, or you will be devoted to the one and despise the other. You cannot serve both God and money" (Matthew 6:24). You can't have faith in two masters.

Peace and satisfaction will always elude you as long as there is a master other than God in your life whom you are pursuing. God won't let you find permanent satisfaction in anything that takes His proper place in your life. Many times these gods are not bad things, they might even be things meant to be a blessing from God. But we've pursued the blessing not the giver of the blessing, and as a result we turned the blessing into a god.

A place in my own life I have struggled to have peace in is my own ability to achieve or accomplish great things. Not that I cared for recognition or status, but somehow my worth became wrapped up in what I could accomplish. The trend began early in my childhood. Being the youngest I always felt I needed to live up to my brothers' sports, art, and business. They seemed to always succeed where I did not. And even though I pursued everything I did with all I had, I never experienced peace or satisfaction. This became a god in my life, a master. And, if I am ever to experience peace in this area, I must cast it aside and find my worth in Christ.

Target Practice

What are you struggling with; Food, money, pleasure, self worth? Are you trying to gain something that you believe will satisfy a longing in your life? Is there a place where you find no lasting peace, or are your actions not in pursuit of God but something else? Take time to identify these gods in your life and talk to someone about them and take the steps to overcome. For sins that have taken root in your life, I strongly urge you to take action through counseling, small group studies and support groups to gain victory in your life.

Chapter 14

LEAP OF FAITH

◎

Because of the service by which you have proved
yourselves, men will praise God for the obedience
that accompanies your confession of the gospel of
Christ, and for your generosity in sharing with them
and with everyone else. 2 Corinthians 9:13

As I mentioned earlier, growing faith can be measured by the amount of peace a person has and by their actions. This action comes from a desire to do what is right before God. Not to earn His love, but because He loves us. It is the actions of gratitude, but there is more to it than that. You see if you believe something, you act on it.

For example, every year my wife buys Christmas gifts way before December even shows up, because she believes Christmas will come on December 25th. She acts in complete confidence that rain or shine, snow or sleet, Christmas is coming on December 25th. In fact, we all know it is coming and so we act on it. Oh we may wait until the 24th to buy presents but we still believe and get ready even if we are not smart about it.

This is the kind of faith I'm talking about. Faith where you trust God and take Him at his Word and act as though it is going to happen just as sure as Christmas is coming on December 25th. The challenge is overcoming our lack of faith because our actions will follow suit. There is a place when we must decide, the moment of truth. Think about it this way. God has made himself known to everyone as it states in Romans 1, but we must decide what we will do with this knowledge. "And without faith it is impossible to please God, because anyone who comes to him must believe that He exists and that He rewards those who earnestly seek Him" (Hebrews 11:6). So we make a decision to trust Him. It is always hard at first until we see God provide and slowly we are assured that He will continue because He always has in the past.

Look at the life of Abraham as it is detailed in Hebrews 11. God starts by asking him to "go to a foreign land." As Abraham sees God provide, God tests him with "give me;" "Sacrifice your son." And Abraham makes the decision that even in this; God will provide. James 2:20-24 points out, Abraham's actions proved his faith. The stark opposite of this is found in Deuteronomy 19, when God leads the Israelites into the desert. He had shown Himself trustworthy, but when the twelve spies are shown the land, they do not have faith

God will provide and they are condemned to wander for forty years.

God will always show Himself to those who seek Him. I love watching new believers as they step out in faith and trust Jesus for salvation. Many times I have seen God overwhelm them with his presence and provision for a 'honeymoon' season, in which they seem to grow quickly. What often happens next is that after this 'honeymoon' season, there comes a time of testing their faith. We see this described in the parable of the four soils.[21] God asks them to go a little further, to step out and act, believing in Him and his word, despite the circumstances they are facing. Jesus says that those who don't develop roots during this time of testing will wither.

This is what it means to live outside your comfort zone. We all want life to be simple, full of peace, but God wants us to experience His power and glory. The reality is life is not simple. It is chaos, constantly going from bad to worse, unless God's power steps in. He brings peace, but in order to overcome this world of chaos we must move forward in our faith. There really is no middle ground. Refusing to continue in what God asks will start you down a road of chaos again. But to step out in faith; to act on what He is leading you to do, will put you in a place of continual dependence on Him. Maybe this is why in Revelation it says there will be no cowards in heaven.[22]

Target Practice

There are probably a few things God has laid on your heart that you are struggling with; things to give up, or things to begin. This book may have brought something to light that you need to start doing, if not now, surely by the time you are done reading. Start small, faith is like a muscle, the more you use it the stronger it become

Chapter 15

SLOT MACHINE PRAYERS
◉

If you remain in me and my words remain in you ask whatever you wish and it will be given you. John 15:7

Prayer and faith go hand in hand. So much so that prayer is of no value without faith. As James puts it,

"But when he asks he must believe and not doubt because he who doubts is like a wave of the sea blown and tossed by the wind. That man should not think he will receive anything from the Lord he is a double minded man unstable in all he does" (James1:6—8).

Prayer has a lot of aspects to it, and there are some great books about strengthening your prayer life. For now I want to look at the simple fact that your prayer life is an evidence of your faith. There are those who pray because it is what you are supposed to do. It is more a religious practice than true communication with God. On a mission trip to Thailand I visited a Buddhist temple. In it was a row of what looked almost like slot machines, where worshippers would put in a coin and it would dispense a prayer. It seems unbelievable that people would believe that could be real, but isn't that what many Christians do? They have exchanged true communication with God to rote phrases they have memorized which they pray without meaning.

Some prayer is worship and praise, but I would dare to say most of our prayers are petitions, asking for something. It is who we are. The big problem with this is that it is usually for our self-comfort. "When you ask you do not receive because you ask with wrong motives that you may spend what you get on your pleasures" (James 4:3). There is nothing that builds our faith more than answered prayers, but so often we pray not according to His will and end up defeated.

"Delight yourself in the Lord and he will give you the desires of your heart" (Psalms 37:4). Many of us read that to mean, "If I obey God then He will give me what I desire." But I would challenge that. As I shared before, my wife likes to buy Christmas presents months in advance. One year she got an incredible deal on t-shirts from a store at the mall. The only problem was the store she bought them from was so new the girls had never heard of it. She then steadily started planting seeds in their heart. Mentioning when others were wearing the same brand and encouraging them to like it. What happened on Christmas day? The girls were thrilled to

92

get the shirts from 'the' store. My wife had planted the desire in their hearts. I believe the same is with this verse. When we seek God and delight ourselves in him, He plants the desires in our heart that only He can fill.

Now God is not against blessing you or making your life easier, but He is not going to provide something in your life that would lead you away from Him. For some of us we pray a lot because our life choices have led us to a place of desperation and constant need of rescue; God does not want his children living defeated lives, so He allows us to live in a place of dependence on Him in order to bring us to our senses. The question is: do you want to live in dependence on him because you believe him for the incredible works of his mighty power? Or, do you want to live in a state of constant desperation because of sinful choices. We will all go through trials. I'd rather go through trials because I believe him for big things!

The truth of the matter is your faith is key to a powerful and effective prayer life. This idea is conveyed in James 5:13-18. God wants to show Himself through his children, but we all too often miss out on His blessings because of our lack of faith in this truth. We become scared. "What if He doesn't show up?" And our lack of faith becomes our downfall.

When Jesus came to his home town He couldn't do many miracles there because of their lack of faith. I don't know about you but I don't want to live there. I think part of the struggle comes from our being over educated. That was the problem in Jesus' home town. They knew Jesus and his family. They had made up their minds about what He could and could not do. Do we play this game? We pray thinking, "I'm not sure if God really wants to do this," so we add in, "Your will" so we're off the hook, but the prayer still sounds good. For years I did this; all the time knowing it was a cop-out. I still wrestle with what God's will is, but I'm learning to expect big things.

To live a prayer life in expectation of big things has been the turning point in my life. It almost seems silly to sweat the small things, the day to day stuff of life. God has always taken care of that stuff. He knows what I need and He has never let me down. Now the fun part is looking for the big things God is doing by looking at what He is placing on my heart. You know those dreams and burdens only He could bring about.

A recent dream God has put on my heart is to have a place where our church could help train church planters, who would in turn start culturally relevant churches in the Northwest. As I was praying about this, God told me through His Spirit, that He wanted me to plant four additional campuses of Outdoorsmen Church throughout the Missoula valley. Now you need to know we are not some superstar church. Starting churches take a lot of resources and we barely make budget. So I asked God for clarification. "God, I have no problem knowing you can provide the resources, but the people I have a hard time with, so if you bring the men, I will do this thing." That week three men called me and said God was leading them to plant a church with us. At that time I hadn't told a soul about my dream. That was only a little over a year ago, and God has brought five couples so far, has provided housing, support and unbelievable opportunities to glorify Him. I anticipate that this thing is bigger than any of us know. Stepping out in faith will do wonders for you prayer life.

Here is the point. Are you praying for just little things or do you trust God for the big things? Your prayer life is part of your faith walk. If you aren't trusting in God for more than the day to day stuff it's time to let God give you a dream bigger than yourself. 'This is to my Father's glory that you bear much fruit, showing yourselves to be my disciples" (John 15:8).

"Fix these words of mine in your hearts and minds; tie them as symbols on your hands and bind them on your foreheads. Teach them to your children, talking about them when you sit at home and when you walk along the road, when you lie down and when you get up. Write them on the doorframes of your houses and on your gates, so that your days and the days of your children may be many in the land the LORD swore to give your ancestors, as many as the days that the heavens are above the earth" (Deuteronomy 11:18—21).

Target Practice

How many times has God answered your prayers? Probably more times than you can count; so try this, it will build you faith. Keep a prayer journal, or better yet, especially if you have children, make a prayer wall. Write down you requests on a sticky note in a way that you will know if it has been answered. In other words, be specific. Put these requests on your prayer wall. Choose one side to be things you are praying for and the other side to be things God has answered. If you start moving things over as God answers them, before you know it, the answered side, along with your faith, will be over flowing.

PART 4:

BALANCED PRIORITIES

Chapter 16:

IT'S NOT ABOUT YOU
◎

For the pagans run after all these things, and your heavenly Father knows that you need them. But seek first his kingdom and his righteousness, and all these things will be given to you as well Matthew 6:32-33

The idea of balanced priorities usually means an equal distribution of time or responsibilities, but life does not flow in equal portions. There is always a demand for more in every area of life. As you know, as soon as you give more to one area, you have to say no to demands in other areas or else run the risk of overloading yourself to the point of falling apart, which consequently causes every area of your life to suffer.

I love hunting but more than that I just love being in the outdoors enjoying God's creation. Unfortunately this can make me a little scary to drive with. More than once I have been distracted by the animals far away, when my wife yells out,

"Look at the animal in the road!"

The problem is my focus is off in the distance and I miss what is standing right in front of me.

What do you do when the unexpected pops up, when there is no balance and things are in chaos? No matter how hard we work at a balanced life, all of us experience times of chaos and times where our focus is out of balance. The problem is when this becomes an ongoing pattern and routine. We need to always have our priorities in focus, so that regardless of what is crying for attention, we will always strive to come back to a place where our priorities line up with God's. When you fail to do this you will find yourself in more and more chaos.

The idea of balanced priorities is not a time management chart, but rather, a way in which to determine what areas of life matter most, and what is being produced in those areas. In other words, life is going to change constantly and if you have not built a solid foundation in the areas that matter, you will find yourself struggling to stay on top when other things demand your attention.

I like to grow things; to see a seed go through the process of becoming a plant to producing something of value: vegetable, fruit or flower. Every plant has its own needs: types of soil and nutrients, temperature, the amount of time until harvest and the amount of water it needs to survive. Some of these are obvious and the need is plain to see. The plant is wilted, you need to water it. Others are not so obvious, like whether the soil needs something in order for the fruit to produce or ripen.

Last summer I grew a bunch of tomatoes. The plants did great! There were other demands on my attention, so as the flowers became tomatoes I didn't notice the brown stripes on the plant's bottom stems, due to a lack of calcium in the soil. If I had, I could have changed the outcome of the later harvest. Instead I grew a great bunch of plants, but the fruit, the important stuff, rotted before it even ripened. It is true heart break when further down the road of life we find our marriages and families have become rotten because we did not give them the priority they needed.

Jesus alluded to this in Matthew when He talked about choices, all the seemingly important stuff people chase after and how our priorities need to be with the things that are truly important.

"So do not worry, saying, 'What shall we eat?' or 'What shall we drink?' or 'What shall we wear?' For the pagans run after all these things, and your heavenly Father knows that you need them. But seek first his kingdom and his righteousness, and all these things will be given to you as well. Therefore do not worry about tomorrow, for tomorrow will worry about itself. Each day has enough trouble of its own" (Matthew 6:31—34).

If our priorities are right, how do you know it? What is the fruit or proof? How do we know whether we are focused on the right areas, or giving the attention where we *need* to give it above all the other things that are vying for our attention. I believe the proof of spiritual maturity in the area of balanced priorities is displayed through our relationships.

Let's face it. The gospel is about what God has done to establish a relationship with us (John 3:16). But it did not stop there. We are told we need to deepen our relationship with God. "Love the Lord your God with all your heart, soul and mind." And then we are to take that to another level by building relationships with others "love your neighbor as yourself."[22] We have been given the "ministry of reconciliation,"[23] which is the restoration of relationships. I love how the Bible describes what our priorities should be which are quite often the very opposite of what the world thinks.

"Do not store up for yourselves treasures on earth, where moths and vermin destroy, and where thieves break in and steal" (Matthew 6:19).

God has made it very clear what He wants His children to be about, so He describes to us in great detail his priorities, which are our relationship with God, family, believers, and non-believers; in that order. It just makes sense that He would desire us to have the same priorities as He does. Many of the priorities we put into our life are temporal. But when we invest in relationships we are investing in eternity. It is just too easy to be sidetracked spending our time investing into everything but relationships. Isn't this a description of the world around us? Remember Jesus said in Matthew 6, "The pagans run after these things." Why? Because it is what they think matters. You might think, "Oh Mark must be an extrovert, he gets a lot of energy from people." But that's not it. In fact, I'm an extreme introvert. I love being alone. Give me a reason, and I could pull away from society all together. At one time that was my plan, to run to Alaska and live off trapping and fishing. God loved me too much, and gave me an extroverted wife instead. As I have grown in my walk with the Lord, I'm all the more convinced that life is about loving and helping other people. This is how we honor God.

> "Then the King will say to those on his right, 'come you who are blessed by my father take your inheritances the kingdom prepared for you since the creation of the world, for I was hungry and you gave me something to eat I was thirsty and you gave me something to drink I was a stranger and you invited me in'... the King will reply, 'I tell you the truth whatever you did for one of the least of these brothers of mine you did for me'" *(Matthew 25:34-35, 40).*

The key to all relationships is the denying of self. A selfish person will never have deep relationships. They will always be about themselves, what they need at the time. In order for any relationship to go deeper you must be willing to give of yourself and look to the needs of others. Even our relationship with God is built on this principle. "Then Jesus said to his disciples, 'if anyone would come after me he must deny himself and take up his cross and follow me for whoever wants to save his life will lose it but whoever loses his life for me will find it'" (Matthew 16:24-25).

When I was young, I was a strong leader. It was nothing for me to take control of a group. My teachers did not care for it much because I got my classmates to do a lot of things they should not have done, such as the time a substitute teacher got mad at me for leaning back in the chair. Within minutes I had convinced the entire class to lean back without even saying a word. She knew what was happening, although she couldn't quite catch us. But, it was evident she knew the ringleader as I got kicked out of class.

As a ten year old I was a gifted salesman who knew how to make a buck. Each day I would go to the grocery store, buy a load of candy and sell it in the lunch line at four times the price. It is amazing how sugar starved kids will pay exorbitant prices to feed their addiction. I would then take my earnings from their lunch money and sell donuts to the construction workers in my neighborhood.

As I matured I began to see in myself the tendency to use people in order to accomplish my goals. Most of my life I have been a leader and this has often given me a false sense of relationship. Part of my own spiritual journey was to begin to cherish relationships not for what they could do for me, but I began to invest in friendships, which has had incredible rewards.

Target Practice

This target practice is literally a target, illustrated below. The center of the target is God and from there the rings move out. What I would like you to do is be honest with yourself. Does the target that you are aiming at have different rings? Things like your job, entertainment or even self. It is hard to hit the mark if you are not even aiming at the right target. Take some time and talk to God about it. Do your passions for life line up with God's target?

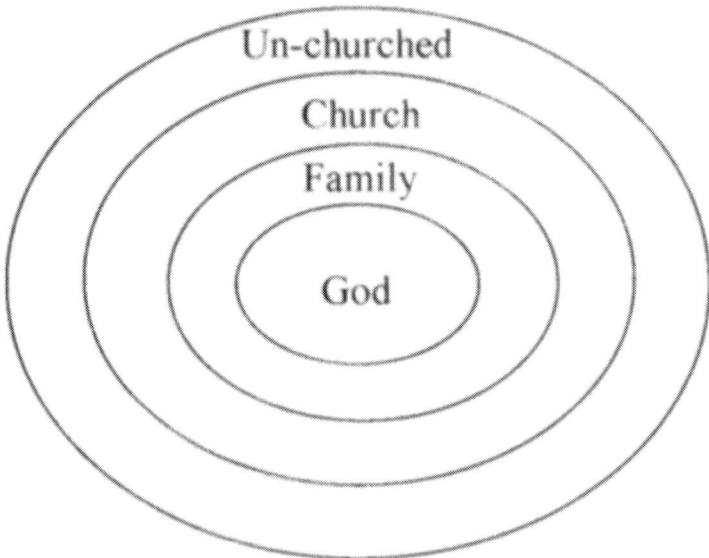

Figure 1 – The rings of relationship priorities[23]

Chapter 17

RELATIONSHIP WITH GOD

◎

If anyone comes to me and does not hate his father and mother his wife and children his brothers and sisters yes even his own life he cannot be my disciple. Luke 14:26.

At first glance the words of Christ seem to say that He does not care about our relationship with others, but this is not what you see throughout the Bible. What He is getting at is; your relationship with Him is of highest priority, even above those whom we should naturally love. It is of such importance that all other relationships are subject to it. It is our top priority. If our relationship with Christ suffers, everything, literally everything, suffers. Christ pointed out in John 15 the only thing that holds us back from the love of God is our willingness to have a love relationship with Him .

Now the great thing about God is He is all in before we are. "While we were still sinners, Christ died for us" (Romans 5:8). In other words our relationship is only as deep as we let it be, we are not waiting on Him. He has done everything to bring us to Him. In Acts 17, Paul points out that God determined the time and exact place you would live in order for you to seek him. As Christians we often promote the fact that it's about a relationship not a religion. We hold to the point that we are now adopted sons and daughters of God Almighty, and have access to Him through Christ, directly to the throne room.

But herein lays the problem. We have access to a Heavenly Father with whom we have built little or no relationship. If Biblical wisdom starts with a fear of God, a holy reverence of His power, our relationship starts with the understanding of His incredible love for us. "And I pray that you, being rooted and established in love, may have power, together with all the Lord's holy people, to grasp how wide and long and high and deep is the love of Christ, and to know this love that surpasses knowledge—that you may be filled to the measure of all the fullness of God" (Ephesians 3:17b-18).

It is important to note that Paul was praying for the Ephesians to grasp this, he does not waste his time praying for things that are not important. The concept of God's love is something we will always struggle to comprehend, because it is so beyond anything we have truly experienced before. We either struggle with grasping his love or receiving it. As I stated earlier, love is the emotion that compels us to do something. It also has the power to draw us closer to someone or something with an ever increasing desire for more. It calms the storm around us as we focus on the object of our incredible love.

This last week as I've been writing this, Sacha and I have been getting ready for our oldest girls to graduate. Now I'm excited for them, as there life is developing, and they start to chase the dreams God has laid on their hearts. But our girls have brought us so much joy, that for the last couple of years we have been mourning the coming change. Even through the busyness of the week, Sacha and I had a chance to get away on a date, nothing big, just dinner at Outback. We picked Outback because of the little two seat booths. We wanted alone time. As the night went on and we talked about all sorts of thing I remember just looking into Sacha's face. The face I know so well, and I was overwhelmed with the feeling of love; knowing that she cared for me as I did for her. I did not want to end that dinner. I could have stayed there forever. I know that regardless of what changes life was going to bring us, we had each other and that was more than enough.

This is the kind of love we are to have with our Heavenly Father. A love that draws us into a place we cannot get enough of; where we have no desire to leave or do other things but to be in His presence; where peace is its strongest because we know not with our minds, but with our hearts, "if God is for us who could stand against us."[24] We need to have a spiritual hunger for God, to fall in love with Him. But we have a tendency to approach our relationship with God from an academic standpoint, trying to know all we can about Him rather than getting to know Him personally. Do not get me wrong; to pursue an understanding of God is a good thing. It should lead you to greater Biblical wisdom, that is, if you apply what you learn of Him. But this is not the love I'm speaking about.

To find this kind of love you have to die to self. When you pursue any relationship with a, "what do I get out of this" mentality, you will receive nothing. You will find that the more you pursue relationships with the mindset of, "how do I give, encourage and genuinely love," then in turn you too will experience love, not necessarily from them but it will come to you all the same. This is true of God as well and exceedingly so in that He will overwhelm you with His love.

So how do you give, encourage and genuinely love God? It is through worship, and by the outpouring of yourself into what matters the most to Him and to others. We will cover others later, for now, how is your worship of God? When Jesus talked about worship, He said, "Yet a time is coming and has now come when the true worshipers will worship the Father in the Spirit and in truth, for they are the kind of worshipers the Father seeks" (John 4:23).

God seeks, or longs, for those who will worship in spirit and truth. Everything else is just religion. Worship is more than just singing, it is how we live our life. But let's start with that overflow of the heart that brings you to a place of heartfelt worship. Does your heart hold intense gratitude and awe towards God? How strong is your response to what God has done for you? This is a good indicator of you current relationship with the Lord. What is it that is holding you back?

The more spiritually mature you are the more you will live a life that can't wait to be in the presence of God. It might be different forms of worship and in different areas such as: crowds, alone in creation or a more traditional, liturgical worship experience that bring us to a place of worship faster. But that is not the issue; it is do you worship in spirit and truth and to what intensity?

What holds you back? What is in the way of a greater relationship with the Lord? Is it not knowing His love for you, or are you unwilling to receive His love. Perhaps it is something you love more than Him and are unwilling to give up. You may not even have what you want, but your desire for it has taken a place over your desire for God. God desperately wants to have a healthy, authentic relationship with us. He does not hold back from us, so if you feel like your worship of Him is lacking ask the Holy Spirit to reveal to you why you are struggling.

When I was in junior high my youth pastor gave a lesson on friendship which has remained true through time. He taught that all relationships are built on three Ts: time, talk and trust. When any one of these is missing the relationship is hindered, sometimes it can maintain for a while if another element is really strong. An example of this is my friendship with people in my home town. We have history together and I trust them and love them deeply but we don't talk too often and the more time passes, the less many of these friendships grow. Some have even disappeared, due to the lack of the three T's. Others have thrived, but it has taken great investment to make them stronger than ever. So you see all three must be present if the relationship is to move forward and grow stronger. If you desire to grow deeper with the Lord, the same is true; you have to build on the three T's.

Target Practice

Take some time to think about what holds you back from worship, and how you are going to change it. How you can work on building the three T's in to your daily life with the Lord. How do you spend time with him? Do you talk to him throughout the day? Do you really trust Him, or are you eaten up with stress and worry? If you don't come up with a plan you will not grow deeper like you should. Relationships take work and intentionality.

Chapter 18:

RELATIONSHIP WITH FAMILY

◎

*If anyone does not know how to manage his own family
how can he take care of God's church?* 1Timothy 3:5

My wedding was quite the experience. I have always been a simple guy with simple tastes. But I was in the United States and the wedding was in New Zealand, so wisely I let my future bride have at it. At the time I didn't realize how much Sacha loved big celebrations. But I was young, in love and couldn't wait to be married. So with 330 guests – five on my side, three pastors officiating the ninety minute, I repeat ninety minute ceremony, everything was ready for her story-book wedding. Apparently God was writing a different story than she planned. During the communion she started to get dizzy, and eventually fainted into the candles. My new mother-in-law jumped up and pulled her veil out of the candles and Sacha got to sit for the rest of the long ceremony. During

the pictures I started to develop flu systems and a high fever.
I couldn't even stand at the reception. Eventually we had to
skip the second reception (I told you my wife celebrates big)
and we were off to our honeymoon with a fever of 106, which
we eventually discovered was typhoid fever. I knew that we
had just committed to 'for better or worse', but we just didn't
expect the worse to happen so quickly!

Our family consists of the people who should know us
best. There is no hiding our weaknesses from them, and they
know our hearts and good intentions. They know whether
we are truly walking with the Lord or whether we are only
trying to look good at church. The health of our family can
be a great indicator of the spiritual health of the leaders of
the home. I say leaders because that could really be anyone
these days. I have seen too many homes run by the children.
It happens mostly where the marriage has fallen apart and
the parents operate in a mode of guilt trying to make up for
the loss, by catering to their kids. Sometimes it just happens
because we feel our children should have the highest priority
in the family. Children are an incredible gift, they exist not to
lead the family but to learn from it, so that one day they may
be able to lead their family in what is right and not be driven
by the common thought of the day.

The point is, God created the family unit to bring about
His glory within us. It is to be a place that fosters unfailing
love, security, and it is to be a training ground to learn how to
handle the world. We as parents are not only to bring up our
children in a way that they understand our values, but that

they see them lived out. Our children are the greatest disciples we will make. They learn so much from us, in good times and bad. They watch how we handle stress; what we value; and how to have a relationship with God in our everyday life. Our children's understanding of their Heavenly Father often is tied to the example and life of their earthly father.

Last summer around a bonfire, a father of one of our youth stated to our youth pastor that he was counting on him to make the difference in his child. Our youth pastor wisely replied,

"I'm plan B, you are plan A."

It is vital that we have other Godly men and women pouring into our kid's lives, but God is first calling on us to do this at home. This is why Paul said, if someone can't manage their home they have no right managing the church.

The priority of the home starts with your spouse not your children. Besides your walk with God, the example of how you love your spouse is the greatest gift you can give your kids. How you love your spouse will determine the kind of marriage they take their cues from later in life as they start theirs. Marriage, like so many things God has ordained, is a physical example of a spiritual concept. Our marriage is to be a representation of our relationship with Christ. "For this reason a man will leave his father and mother and be united to his wife and the two will become one flesh. This is a profound mystery but I am talking about Christ and the church" (Ephesians 5:31-32).

All through Ephesians 5:22-6:4, Paul talks about the family, in light of our relationship with Christ. Knowing what great lengths God has come to have a relationship with us and what He promises to do for our sake, it leads me to believe that His desire is for you to have an incredible marriage. In a time when marriages are falling apart all over, what greater way to show the world God's love than through the incredible love you have for your spouse. If you can't love your spouse how can you truly love someone you don't know?

Now some of you have had some pretty rough marriages. I know your spouse can be a jerk and has hurt and wronged you. This is not right and not what is intended. If you feel that you are in a bad marriage, don't put it off, you must get help. Diligently work on your marriage relationship and do what it takes to bring it to a healthy place. God uses marriage as an example of what our relationship with Him is to be like, but He also uses a bad marriage to show how long suffering He is. The Old Testament book, Hosea, depicts the story of a man whom God instructs to marry an adulterous wife. God uses Hosea's marriage to show the people how great His love is for them and to what length He will go to keep the relationship. Many of the hardships we go through in marriage are for our refinement, that we will grow up and not be so driven by selfishness or stubbornness.

Sacha is my opposite in personality. The first couple of years of our marriage were rough, to say the least. We cared for each other but we did not understand each other at all. I was the youngest of three brothers, my sister moved out when I was young. My parents divorced when I was thirteen and I lived with my Dad. I understood the world of men. On the other hand; Sacha grew up with a very capable mother, younger sister and a white collar, gentleman father.

Most marriages deal with differences in communication, but when you marry someone from another country, miscommunication multiplies! Imagine the uncomfortable looks we'd get when my wife would enter a family's home and comment on how much she liked their pot plants.

Our differing backgrounds played a huge role in our misunderstandings, even in the way we handled conflict not to say anything about how we communicated. But it was those differences that I needed in my life to help me grow. As a young man I had a tendency to lead strong and run over people without knowing it. Sacha helped me see that, and helped me change my passion to achieve, into a passion to see others achieve. She truly has been my 'iron sharpening iron'.

But God did not think that was enough, He also gave me three girls to raise. They are the joy of my life, and they too have done their fair share of shaping me to be more like Christ. From simple things like how to listen and pay attention (do you know how much *more* girls talk than boys?), to deep things like overcoming my fear and trusting God with their lives as they have traveled overseas to do missions. I would not be the man I am today if it wasn't for my family. And not just for the support and love, but also the grace to work through the rough and raw moments of life.

"Religion that God our Father accepts as pure and faultless is this: to look after orphans and widows in their distress and to keep oneself from being polluted by the world" (James 1:27). I think it is interesting that the church is told they must take care of the widows and orphans first. In other words, family is so important to God that the church is mandated to care for those who do not have a family. One of the greatest blessings God has given us is opening the doors of our home to kids that have not been raised in the healthiest of homes. Several of them now serve alongside of us in ministry and some we have truly adopted in our hearts as our own.

You may well be the only believer in your family because your spouse has no interest in Christ at all. This does not mean you are off the hook, regardless of their beliefs. We must give our family high priority because it has the greatest potential for spiritual impact on them.

> "Wives, in the same way submit yourselves to your own husbands so that, if any of them do not believe the word, they may be won over without words by the behavior of their wives, when they see the purity and reverence of your lives" (1 Peter 3:1-2).

If you are single, your role plays out differently. But it is still your priority to make your family come only after your relationship with God. Christ even got mad at the Pharisees for allowing children to pledge their help to God before their parents, because by doing so, they were in essence breaking the commandment of honoring their mother and father. If you have a godly family, count your blessings. If not, hold on for

God may be using you to be instrumental in bringing your family to Him. Your role, declared in scripture, is one that is to honor and obey your parents. This may sound old fashioned, but it will literally change the outcome of your life. In time, and it is not really that long, you may have your own family to lead and your relationship with God will still need to be number one. When you fall in love with your future spouse, it is much more challenging to keep God as first priority in your life than you can ever imagine, which is why so many marriages struggle.

Target Practice

The family should be a place where the fruit of the Spirit is seen at all times. The home should be a sanctuary from the world; a place of peace and security where your spouse and children see and experience the love of Christ flowing through you. The relationship you have with your family only comes second to your relationship with God. Only when these relationships are healthy and in order should we focus on our next relationship priority.

As you know this book is not going to help you achieve maturity in every area of life, but rather its goal is to focus on areas of life that measure our spiritual maturity. There are many great resources on achieving a godly marriage. Know this, it takes work to die to self and live for someone. But I know that God's desire is for you to have an incredible marriage, because it brings Him glory as two become one.

Chapter 19

RELATIONSHIP WITH BELIEVERS

◎

So Christ himself gave the apostles, the prophets, the evangelists, the pastors and teachers, to equip his people for works of service, so that the body of Christ may be built up until we all reach unity in the faith and in the knowledge of the Son of God and become mature, attaining to the whole measure of the fullness of Christ. Ephesians 4:11 — 13

Our relationship with believers is of great importance when we are talking about spiritual maturity. In Ephesians 4 there are several points that come out that are attributed to our spiritual maturity. One of them is: being prepared for works of service, which we will talk about in the sacrificial service chapter. First, let's look at the idea of "reaching unity." Unity is what we find Christ praying for on his last night in John 17:20-23 as He prays for the church to come, "that all of them may be one," and this is meant to be a witness to the world.

Now before you go getting upset about "that" denomination, or the church that did "such and such," let's just start with ourselves. Throughout the years I have come across countless individuals who know and love God but can't stand the church and are not in a body of believers for one reason or another. This is not Christ's plan or desire for you, and in the same way, neither is going to a church that you do nothing but attend. I ran across a gal the other day who informed me that her church was an internet church and it was all she needed. Granted you can find some good teaching through the countless media outlets, but teaching is only one part of what the church is about .We were meant to be engaged in each other's lives.

As the old joke goes: a man was stranded on a deserted Pacific island for years. Finally one day a boat sailed into view. The man frantically waved to draw the skipper's attention, and the boat came near the island.

When the sailor reaches the island he greets the stranded man and asks him, "What are those three huts you have here?"

"Well, that's my house there," said the island dweller.

"What's that next hut?" asks the sailor.

"I built that hut to be my church," exclaimed the man.

"What about the other hut," asked the sailor.

"Oh, that's where I used to go to church."[25]

Unity is easy to keep by yourself. It is when you engage with others that the struggle becomes apparent. And the struggle is purposeful because it helps us grow. It is the spiritually immature who come up with reasons to pull away from the church. Now there may be a legitimate reason one must leave a certain church, but no matter how great the pain, one needs to be in a church in order to find healing and health.

Unity is not finding a closed group of people who believe the exact same thing, but rather, God's plan was to unify people with different backgrounds; understandings and life experiences to work together to find the truth of God's Word. To strive to encourage one another to become more Christ-like. This scenario is certainly not the most likely way to create unity. Maybe that is why unity is meant to be a witness to the world. Proverbs 27:17 says, "As iron sharpens iron so one man sharpens another." You realize that in order for one iron object to sharpen another, they do have to come in contact with each other. And not only that, it must be in an abrasive way in order to do any good.

So, in order to keep unity with so much diversity, even with the common ground of Christ, it takes a dying of self and a love for others. This can truly only come from the work of the Holy Spirit flowing through you. This is one of the reasons I believe participation in church is linked to spiritual maturity.

"And He gave the apostles, the prophets, the evangelists, the shepherds and teachers, to equip the saints for the work of ministry, for building up the body of Christ, until we all attain to the unity of the faith and of the knowledge of the Son of God, to mature manhood, to the measure of the stature of the fullness of Christ" (Ephesians 4: 11—13).

The passage we started the chapter with, not only speaks to service and unity, but also to the building up of each other in the knowledge of Christ, through the system God put together. Look at it again. Note that the verse starts off by listing different spiritual leaders of the church, giving the reason it is their job to help the church reach spiritual maturity. If you ever wonder what the role of your pastor is; this passage delivers the Biblical definition or job description. I also see a structure that is talked about throughout Scripture which the church is to be a part of, but has regrettably let slide.

Most of us know the Great Commission, "Therefore go and make disciples of all nations, baptizing them in the name of the Father and of the Son and of the Holy Spirit, and teaching them to obey everything I have commanded you. And surely I am with you always, to the very end of the age" (Matthew 28:19-20). We know it, but we don't really fulfill it. Nowadays there is this whole debate over, "make disciples." The very word "disciple" confuses people today. We know God has called us to make disciples, but what is that and what does it look like? We get overwhelmed before we even try. So let's take a different look at "teaching them to obey everything I have commanded."

I am sure you know a few things about the Lord and what He desires for your life. So what holds you back from sharing with someone else? Most of us all want a mentor in our life. Someone who cares for us constantly, holds us accountable, and helps us to find the right way, but we don't like the idea of being a mentor for others. Before you write it all off, look at this verse, "You then, my son be strong in the grace that is in Christ Jesus. And the things you have heard me say in the presence of many witnesses entrust to able men who will also be qualified to teach others" (2 Timothy 2:1-2).

Now, put all three verses together, and you will see that our churches are a gathering place for people to mentor, disciple and lead others in the pursuit of spiritual maturity. So there are three levels of relationships that need to happen. We should strive to have someone more mature than us mentoring us in the way of Christ; keeping us accountable in our relationship with God, and challenging us so we do not stray or become complacent individuals. Secondly, we are to have friends that encourage us and whom we encourage through the day to day of life. Additionally, we are to have someone whom we mentor and help become more mature as we encourage them on the path of seeking God. Regardless of where you start in these roles you will find that in a healthy mentoring relationship you will mutually encourage and teach each other as you grow together to become more like Christ.

Going to church and listening to a sermon does not equate to your having a mentor in your life. Nor does the fact that you have been walking with Christ a long time disqualify you from needing a mentor in your life. In fact I have seen the more spiritually mature someone becomes, the more they strive to have others speak into their life and keep them accountable. As time goes by there is always the danger for spiritual temptations to creep in, like pride and complacency toward spiritual things. A good mentor keeps us seeking God's will and stepping out of our comfort zone to push ahead. They believe not so much in us as in the purpose that has been given to us to be more then we currently are.

God has blessed me with many mentors over the years. Some have been for a short season of maturing and growth weaving in and out of my life for specific seasons of ministry. Others have walked the journey with me for years.

Many Christians have never had a mentor, but having someone that mentors you is vital. It means that you have time with someone whom you can talk through things in your life that need to be discussed one on one. We need to realize that we will never have a mentor that meets all of our needs. God made us all different parts of the body for a reason. He will not allow just one person to sharpen or refine you, to be healthy it needs to be many.

So what are the keys to finding a mentor? First we must have a teachable and humble spirit. No one wants to invest time in a know it all. People want to feel like their time is valuable to you and that you are willing to put into practice what you are learning.

In order to have a mentor you are going to have to ask. As you have been reading this book there are hopefully some areas that you would like to work on in your spiritual walk, to gain some victory. Pick someone you see has the qualities you desire and just ask them if you could have coffee sometime. Don't ask for a long term commitment, just shoot for the first gathering and see how it goes. When you get together share what you see in them how you wish you were stronger in that area, and ask whether they would meet with you on a regular basis to talk and keep each other accountable and to read scripture and pray. If they are the right one for you they will be honored you asked.

I believe that since mentoring is so vital to our spiritual maturity, Satan is not going to want it to succeed. The steps are simple, but you will have to fight to make them work. It will be a battle in ways you can't imagine. But it is well worth it and will bring true life transformation.

Now having Christian friends is usually not as hard as finding a mentor, but for some of us we just have not put the time in or we have been around the wrong friends. The key is to have friends that encourage you in your faith, people who understand what you are going through in life and just love to be together. Most healthy churches are doing this through small group Bible Studies. Small churches have an easier time feeling like family, where everyone knows each other, but even then it is too easy to put on a good front. In most large churches you will find that small home groups are the focus point. It is the only way to make sure people are connecting to each other. This is where people feel loved and cared for. If someone is hurting, a good small group will rally around them to take care of them as much as they can. Depending on the spiritual maturity of the leaders, the group can often get more out of their time together because it is geared to where they are as individuals with an element of transparency and accountability. The true key to the success of these groups is their love for each other, their friendship.

Twenty some years ago Sacha and I were involved in a small group for young married couples. Some of them were friends that I had grown-up with, but nearly everyone in our group, after twenty years, still reaches out to each other, even across states, because of the love we found being together. I think every one of us goes to a different church now, but we are friends for life.

The problem most of us have is we don't like putting ourselves out there. We feel a little lonely but not enough to risk being rejected. Or we simply might think it takes too much work to make new friends, and we just don't have time for that. The truth of the matter is; we need each other more than we know. Not only as help mates in our spiritual maturity, but also for the love and joy that motivates us to be better people. So reach out and begin to surround yourself with friends that will encourage you toward greater things.

If Jesus commanded us to make disciples, why are we not? Before you say, but I have never been discipled, I would ask you how are we going to break the trend of Christians growing up without being discipled if we don't start discipling others? The Holy Spirit will help you through. To take the responsibility for others to grow spiritually is the big step from adolescence to adulthood. I know there are people in your life who need your help to continue on the right path.

"Instead, speaking the truth in love, we will grow to become in every respect the mature body of him who is the head, that is, Christ. From him the whole body, joined and held together by every supporting liga-ment, grows and builds itself up in love, as each part does its work" (Ephesians 4:15-16).

If we don't obey Jesus in making disciples, we are not doing our part to help the body grow and build itself up in love. Don't make it hard. Ask someone you know that could use some encouragement or direction in their life and meet them for lunch or coffee. Do something fun together a few times to build trust and friendship, then see if they would be up to meeting at a regular time once a week, or at least once every other week to talk about life and their spiritual walk. From there, see if they would be willing to read through a portion of the Bible together and discuss what you are both getting out of it. Don't make it more complicated than that. And if they don't want it, move on to the next person the Holy Spirit puts on your heart.

Books are great but they are not the Word of God. The Holy Spirit speaks through the Word of God and you want the Spirit's speaking more than others. Try to stay with the Bible and only use other books as a reference. After the first time, give them a journal to write down what they are learning or have questions about. You will find that it is mostly questions about things they don't understand, which often leads to great discussions. Encourage them to share what the Spirit revealed to them. He is teaching them to listen and anticipate the Spirit speaking that will get them excited about the Word of God.

During my discipleship meetings I don't come with a planned discussion, but rather seek to understand what is happening in their life and where the Spirit is leading. I do listen to see if I can pick up on a recurring theme or idea being shared, which points to one of the five areas of spiritual maturity, so I know what someone needs help with in order to reach the next step. It's not hard; you just need to do it.

Target Practice

There are three relationships that we need to have with believers: building friendships, mentoring those in need and being mentored ourselves. The more intentional you are about making them healthy the healthier you will become. Take some time to come up with a plan to be more involved in other's lives and less busy in what does not matter long term. Also write out a list of characteristics your ideal mentor would have and see if you can be that for someone else.

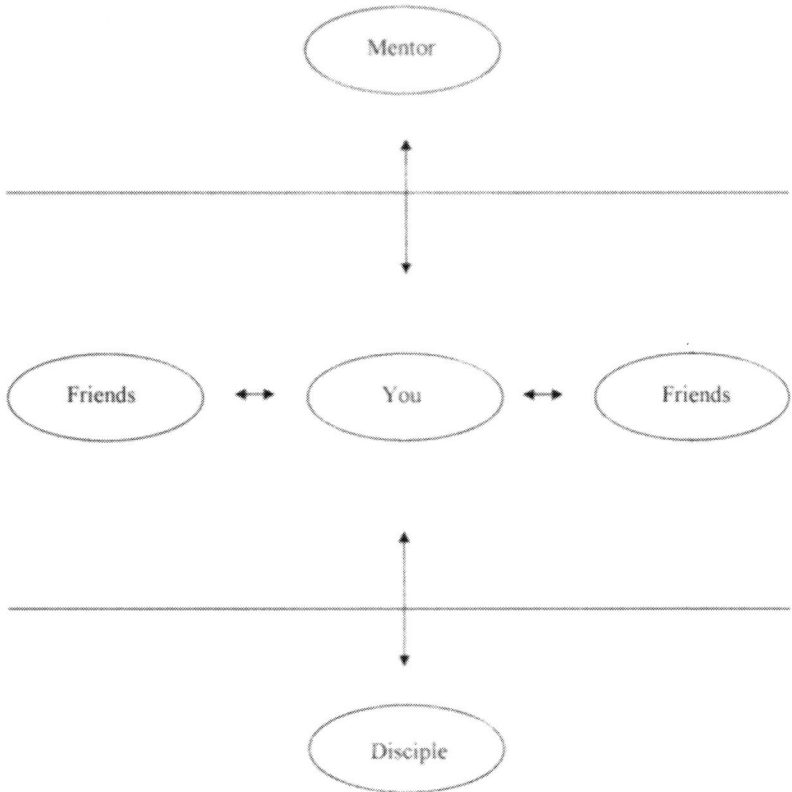

Figure 2 – Discipleship Graph[26]

Chapter 20

RELATIONSHIP WITH UNBELIEVERS

◎

Be wise in the way you act toward outsiders; make the most of every opportunity. Colossians 4:5-6

When it comes to unbelievers, we know we are to be evangelists — well maybe not. Let me explain. A couple of years ago we did a survey of our church to see what we as a church were strong in, and what we needed to strengthen. One of the questions had to do with evangelism. I try hard not to use Christian words or terminology too much, but I was surprised when one of our leaders came up front to ask me what evangelism meant. She had already led her husband to the Lord and was quite the witness at work; she just did not know that the church had come up with a word to describe what she was already doing.

I think for those who have been in the church for a long time, evangelism and being a witness for Jesus is one of the scariest things to do. Probably because of one or more of the following reasons: We have turned it into, or have been told it is a system in which we walk up to a stranger and ask, or rather tell them a series of prefabricated questions they didn't ask in the first place in order to get them to repeat after you a scripted prayer. The second problem we have is; we don't believe that anyone is really interested. Thirdly, we don't have unbelieving friends. We have pulled away from unbelievers because we believed they would lead us astray. Plus the more we hang out at church, the more our friendships are centered at church and we just find that our old relationship have faded away.

If you look at Colossians 4:5-6 again, "Be wise in the way you act toward outsiders; make the most of every opportunity. Let your conversation be always full of grace seasoned with salt, so that you may know how to answer everyone." Paul is talking about living a life of intentionality with unbelievers. Not only are we to live in a way that our conversations would be pleasant, but that they would ask us. I don't know about you but I don't tend to ask strangers about something unless I know they are an expert on something. I do, however, ask my friends what they think about things all the time, even when I know they don't have all the answers. They're my friends, why wouldn't I ask them what they think.

Here's the point: I think we are to live in a way that makes friends with others, which takes intentionality. It is a lot of work to make new friends. In other words: be the first to initiate conversation, be generous, and show concern and interest in others. All of this takes a dying to self. It takes effort but it is how we are to live toward unbelievers. We need to be about making friends first.

The book, *I Once Was Lost: What Postmodern Skeptics Taught Us about Their Path to Jesus* by Don Everts and Doug Schaupp shows most unbelievers go through four steps before coming to a place of surrender to the Lord. The first three steps have to do with an unbeliever's relationship with a believer.

The first step occurs when a believer earns an unbelievers trust. Trust is a key to any relationship. There is often a mistrust of Christians due to media portrayal, and the many bad experiences un-believers have had with either a church or a so called believer. But, if a unbeliever knows you are a believer in Christ, they want to know if you really care about them first. If you feel like you need to present the gospel first, they will write you and Christ off. Trust is built by being a true friend.

The second is when curiosity is built by a believer's way of living. This means that you have to spend enough time with them in order for them to notice you are different. It also means you have to live a different lifestyle than those who do not believe in Christ. I don't recommend dressing like the Amish in order to do this; what should be different is your character. It is what people see and it is the fruit of the Spirit that people are attracted to.

The third is when a unbeliever desires change because they have seen it in their believing friend. You will find that unbelievers long to have purpose and hope in their life and to be set free from things that hold them back. And if you have been a true friend they will try to mimic much of your life in the hope of having what you have. This is the time to help them understand that you are different, not because you are self-disciplined but because it is the work of the Lord in you that makes you different.[27]

Like all things, we like to make it harder than it really is or try and explain it all out in detail. To me, the Bible is clear — we are to live a life of intentionality with others. When it comes to unbelievers, we are to do our best to be great friends. If you are becoming more like Christ day by day, full of truth and grace, unbelievers will either have nothing to do with you or they will want what you've got. But they have to be in your life for this to take place.

To be a friend you must be true to who you are. Don't change to fit in and don't be something you're not to show you're a believer. Both reactions are not good and are harmful to you and others spiritually. Putting on a mask will only leave you with no true friendships. If the way in which your unbelieving friend lives becomes an area of temptation, or a stumbling block, I would suggest pulling away from the relationship so as to not shipwreck your own spiritual life. You shouldn't look at investing into others until you can handle the temptations some unbelieving friends may bring. Personally, I abstain from anything that may make it hard for others to see Christ first, even if I have the freedom in it and do not wrestle with the temptation.

Target Practice

Don't make unbelievers your 'project', just be a great friend. You should have a couple of unbelieving friends and if you don't it's time to reach out. Did you ever think spiritual maturity could be measured by your friendships with unbelievers? God did. That is all Christ had to hang out with and He loved them. How can we be like Him if we don't love who He loved?

PART 5:

GODLY CHARACTER

Chapter 21

WHO IS THE REAL YOU?
◎

And we all, who with unveiled faces contemplate the Lord's glory, are being transformed into his image with ever-increasing glory, which comes from the Lord, who is the Spirit. 2 Corinthians 3:18

It is important to understand when I'm talking about character; I'm not talking about personality. A person's personality seldom changes unless a major life event occurs in which a person finds they must change in-order to survive emotionally; this is seldom healthy. Personality and character are two different things. Personality speaks of the uniqueness of a person; how they see and perceive things, and their general response to their environment. A basic personality profile looks at whether a person is people or task driven, as well as whether they are fast paced or pay more attention to detail. More in-depth personality profiles will look at creativity or whether a person makes decisions off of fact or feeling. All these things are good for us to know about ourselves and it definitely can be a tool to help us understand others. God has created all of us different and although certain cultures may value one personality type over another, the truth of the matter is the vast differences in personalities speaks to God's incredible glory in creation.

Character on the other hand is different. Two people with the same personality can have completely opposite characters. In addition, one's character can change. This is what it means to become more like Christ. It's not that our personalities are all to become the same, like clones, but rather our character is to imitate Jesus. Paul even went as far as saying, "Imitate me as I imitate Christ" (1 Corinthians 11:1).

Character is an outward expression of the heart. It can be seen in opposites like anger and love, fear and boldness, forgiveness and grudges. Several times the Bible lists sinful behaviors to be replaced by godly character. These lists are defined as the desires of our heart. You may think that sinful behavior is not an expression of our character, but it is. The truth of the matter is our character is the outflow of our heart.

"Make a tree good and its fruit will be good or make a tree bad and its fruit will be bad for a tree is recognized by its fruit, you brood of vipers. How can you who are evil say anything good? For out of the overflow of the heart the mouth speaks, the good man brings good things out of the good stored up in him

137

and the evil man brings evil things out of the evil stored up in him" (Matthew 12:33—35).

Godly character should be one of the easiest proofs of our spiritual maturity. But the problem is we do not associate sinful behavior with character. On top of that, everyone we run into has the ability to be loving, passionate and kind. Even Jesus said unbelievers know how to love those who are good to them. But Jesus took it a step further and pointed to our character when He asked us to love our enemies, those who would mistreat us. Jesus was speaking about a greater love than is in the world. Jesus spoke of a love so strange that others would know without a doubt those who had it were his disciples.

In Acts 6 we see Stephen had this kind of love; love that could forgive the men, as they cast the stones which killed him. It is written about Stephen that he was a man full of the Holy Spirit. You can see it through the miracles he was doing, the wisdom he had when confronted by the Sanhedrin, and definitely through his character, namely his love. I believe when Paul was writing "And we who with unveiled faces, all reflect the Lord's glory are being transformed into his likeness with ever-increasing glory which comes from the Lord who is the Spirit" (2 Corinthians 3:18), he was thinking about Stephen; How his face was like that of an angel as he was being accused in Act 6:15.

It is funny, because I have never really thought about God's glory physically revealing itself in my face because

I was becoming more like him. Though I can recall many people, who after they received Christ as their Savior, their countenance immediately changed. Their face revealed a look of joy and peace that was not there before.

Godly character is far more than being good to each other. It compels us to do extraordinary things; much like the early church who were so devoted to each other they met every day. They honestly could not get enough of each other. It's like falling in love when you can't wait to be together again.

We say we love the people at our church, but when was the last time you had them over for dinner? Now imagine every night going and hanging out with someone. Most of us would say, "no way," but that is just it, the early church had a love for each other that made it what they desired. Their love was evident in the fact that they were selling things in order to help one another out. Heck, we only do that for our children, because we love them. If you think about it, it's no wonder God added to their numbers. Who wouldn't be drawn to a group of loving people like that?

Godly character is one of the best evangelistic tools out there; more so than knowing all the right words. When you live a life that is so different than the world, people notice and they will be drawn to the gospel that actually works to change us. Much of the church looks like the world, not the image of Christ, because our character has not changed.

In 1 Peter 2:11 we are told we are aliens in this world; in Romans 12:2 it reads, "Do not conform to the pattern of this world, but be transformed by the renewing of your mind.

Then you will be able to test and approve what God's will is—
his good, pleasing and perfect will."

When my daughters were little, I made the mistake of
watching an alien cartoon spoof with them. Subsequently for
six months my eldest daughter Hannah was terrified at the
thought of aliens. She would drive us crazy asking,

"Are aliens real?" Breakfast, lunch and dinner, she'd
persist!

Repeatedly we told her, "Aliens aren't real." But, despite
our reassurance she was consumed with fear. And then, one
day her fears were realized when we crossed the Canadian
border. Sacha is a New Zealander, so when the patrol officer
asked her if she was a US citizen, she calmly replied,

"No I'm a resident alien, here is my card".

I wish you could have seen my kid's faces as they stuttered,

"Mo-mo-mommy, you never told us you were an alien."

When we are no different than the world we have a form
of godliness, but deny its power. That power comes from the
Holy Spirit. When we give in to our sin nature we quench the
power of the Holy Spirit in us. I have had dear friends who
have walked for a long time in things they knew God was
asking them to give up. The sad part about it is this road will
inevitably lead them to a place where they no longer can hear
the Spirit's voice or guidance.

Target Practice

It's time to be honest about who you are. A good friend
told me the other day that maturity stops when someone

becomes prideful because they begin to live in a false reality. When someone lives in a false reality, they no longer make decisions based on truth, therefore they stop maturing. I agree, for Jesus said the truth will set you free. So it is time to deal with the truth of how you act when tough things happen. Don't blame or use your circumstances, as to why you act the way you do, they are only a mirror of your true heart. So I ask you, who are you?

Chapter 22

WHAT'S LOVE GOT TO DO WITH IT
◎

But the fruit of the Spirit is love, joy, peace, patience, kindness, goodness, faithfulness gentleness, and self-control; against such things there is no law... Since we live by the Spirit let us keep in step with the Spirit. Galatians 5:22, 25

Love, how can we go wrong with more love? Love fulfills the two greatest commandments. Love God, love others. One of the major themes of the Bible is love and how we are so limited without it. Many of our acts can look like we are a good Christ follower, but without love it is only empty religion. I love the way Paul puts it in Galatians 5:6, "The only thing that counts is faith expressing itself through love."

Don't forget, "There is no law against love," for it is the fulfillment of the law. Think about what that really means.

Every sinful thing that we do is in direct opposition to love. If our love was strong enough we would not sin. Take any sin and get to the root. I think you will see that love is what is missing. Love is the key to becoming like Christ.

There is a lot of denominational debate about the proof of the Holy Spirit in a believer. Fruit is another word for proof, and as you well know (so much so that you probably skimmed over the opening verse) the fruit, or proof, of the Spirit is everything that we would say makes up Godly character, starting with love. Really, the way Galatians 5:22 is written, everything that follows; joy, peace, patience, kindness, goodness, faithfulness, gentleness, self-control, is all a part of love. I added verse 25, because I think staying in tune with the Holy Spirit is what most of us wrestle with the most.

I don't think anyone would argue the fact that godly character has to do in part with our ability to love. Our struggle lies with the idea that our sin nature is what reveals our true character; or, the lack of the Holy Spirit's control in our lives. What else would Paul be referring to? If you read Galatians 5 in context, to give way to the desires of our sin nature is to not keep in step with the Holy Spirit. To keep in step with the Holy Spirit is to have the attributes of love in our life.

"By this everyone will know that you are my disciples, if you love one another" (John 13:35). And later, Jesus says in John 15:8, "This is to my Father's glory, that you bear much fruit, showing yourselves to be my disciples." What is the fruit of the Spirit? You cannot deny that our ability to love is a proof of the Spirit and as well, a proof of belonging to

Christ. Oh, and by the way Jesus said that it was to God's *glory* that we bear much fruit.

The fact that bearing fruit is to God's glory is a great relief. It is something God desires to bring about in us, so He is faithful and will provide the outpouring of the Spirit in us to be conformed to the image of Christ. We cannot make it happen, but we can stop it from happening. As we continue to grow in our Biblical wisdom and obedience toward God, not giving in to sin, the outpouring of the Spirit will be in our life.

Target Practice

There are three things you should do from time to time in order to grow in the fruit of the spirit. First, what sin are you not dealing with? Confess it, seek help and/or accountability. Set up protection from the temptation of it. Begin to see it for what it is; a dam that is blocking the outpouring of the Spirit in your life. Secondly, pray for the renewing of your mind toward the ungodly things in your life. Ask that you would have greater love in all areas of your life.

Paul tells the church to increase or do more and more in acts of love and other areas of godly character. So, there is a place for us to be looking for opportunities to do the things that please the Lord. And finally, take some time every week to think about how you could excel in love toward others and act on it.

Chapter 23

LIFE IS PAIN
◉

Not only so, but we also rejoice in our sufferings, because we know that suffering produces perseverance, perseverance character and character hope.
Romans 5:3-4

Refining our character never sounds good. It reminds me of my wrestling coach in Junior High. He would always say things like, "no pain, no gain," and, "what doesn't break you only makes you stronger." He seemed to have a sick addiction to making people hurt. I have always hated those kinds of sayings. I would much rather have pleasures in my life over pain. It is why I avoid the dentist with a passion. Just the thought of the drill fills me with dread.

Going through hard times and suffering is not something we go looking for, so long as we are mentally healthy. I have seen a good number of people who seem to look for drama and stress because they don't know what to do with themselves if they don't have something crazy happening in their lives. This is unhealthy and usually a sign of abuse in the past that needs to be dealt with. God is a God of peace and rest. He gave us the Sabbath day as a sign of things to come, namely salvation and heaven.

But, as Westley from *The Princess Bride* would say,

"Life is pain, Highness. Anyone who says differently is selling something."[28]

There is something to the fact that we all go through pain one way or another, but much of our suffering is of our own making. Like John Wayne's character, Sergeant Stryker said in Sands of Iwo Jima,

"Life is tough, but it's tougher if you're stupid."[29]

If you are doing things you know you shouldn't, God's going to bring consequences into your life to help you figure it out. Like touching a hot stove, you only have to do it once to find out it's not a good idea. It is those things that have been happening for a long time with seemingly no consequence you need to think about. If you think you are getting away with it, it either means you are not God's child, so He is not disciplining you in love, or the consequences are going to be so big they will likely reshape your life. You don't want to go there, trust me. Suffering from our sin is kind of a wake-up call that says, "God wants more for us than the mud pies we so love to make and play in."

"My son, do not make light of the Lord's discipline, and do not lose heart when He rebukes you, because the Lord disciplines the one He loves, and He chastens everyone He accepts as His son" (Hebrews 12:5-6). There is other suffering that comes our way, much of which is out of our control and only a solid faith will overcome. It is in these moments our true character is revealed. Many of us have the tendency to blame our circumstances for our lack of character. Often I've heard people say, "I'm not actually like this, but it's what I'm going through that is making me this way." We fall into the trap where we don't feel responsible for our reactions. To do this is like looking at the mirror and blaming it for the dirt on our face. Suffering removes our blinders and reveals what is normally hidden, often even from ourselves.

This is why it is good to know yourself. For example, it has taken me over a year to write this book. Despite God's clear direction to write the book, I made many excuses and have been dragging my feet. Last week marked the start of Montana's archery elk season; the one month I long for all year. Do I write or go hunting? That is a dumb question, hunt of course! On the third day I had two massive bulls bugling and fighting below me. If you have never heard or seen elk do this you are missing out on one of the greatest things in nature. I ran down the mountain just in time to see the bigger one chase the loser away. In my excitement I lost my footing and twisted my ankle. I spent the next four hours dragging myself through the woods half in the pitch dark; searing pain in every step, unwilling to stop knowing that if I did it would probably become my final resting place. Finally, I made it the three miles back to the road and eventually home. I wrestled with God.

"Why? I'm a good man," I thought to myself. (The, "I'm good, so bad things shouldn't happen to me," mentality). When the doctor told me it would take a month to heal, and I needed to stay off it completely for one week, I heard God say, "Now you can write that book for me."

I hate the fact that my character would jump to thinking I'm something special, that I should be exempt from suffering, and that I again needed a swift kick to focus on what He had asked me to do. I pray that God will use this book to strengthen His kingdom. But I know that it will probably do more for me than anyone.

"Not only so, but we also glory in our sufferings, because we know that suffering produces perseverance; perseverance, character; and character, hope" (Romans 5:3-5). How we handle suffering reveals our character, but the trick is to allow suffering to mold us to become something more than we were before. Just because someone goes through pain doesn't necessarily mean they've produced character. It is our ability to learn from the pain, and to get victory over our weaknesses, that produces character. According to the verse above, when we grow in Godly character, hope grows within us. The true pain of suffering is the lack of hope. So if we want to get victory through our suffering, we must be diligent to overcome.

One of the greatest refiners in our life is other people. The whole idea of two people becoming one is the changing of our character in order to live as one. The more we are around someone, the more we become alike.

If we can see it in older folks who have been married for a long time and in families where the children tend to do the same things because they have the same value system as their parents, shouldn't we expect it to happen in our relationship with God? The more we walk with Christ, and the more we understand the Lord, the more we should become like Him.

Some of the people the Lord puts into our life are brought in, in order to shape us, our passions, and our temperament. You know who I mean. We see them as an irritant. These may include your spouse, but it is one of the greatest ways God molds and shapes our character. It is hard to love some people, but that is what God has called us to; to die to self and love all God puts in our path.

Target Practice

What does your character say about God in your life? Who are some of the people you need to show a Christ-like character? What suffering in your life has brought about a better understanding of who you are?

CHAPTER 24

THE RIGHT STUFF
◎

Now the overseer is to be above reproach, faithful to his wife, temperate, self-controlled, respectable, hospitable, able to teach, not given to drunkenness, not violent but gentle, not quarrelsome, not a lover of money. 1 Peter 3:2-3

I have seen so many churches looking to hire new leadership who look first to the education and experience of the new hire, and completely assume the godly character of a leadership candidate. Many times they don't even bother to call references. They reason, "They must have Godly character or they would not be in ministry." Later they pay the price as the leader reveals their true self over time, often hurting many people on the way.

Character was one of the first things looked for in the early church; although, it was stated differently. They asked for those who were full of the Holy Spirit, which I believe is evident through your character.

If character is what the early church was looking at in-order to appoint or confirm an overseer; how important should it be to us? The leadership of the church sets the example of how we are to live our life. If there is a standard our leadership is supposed to have, then why would we settle for anything less? Proverbs is full of verses talking about avoiding people of bad character; such as those who gossip, lie, are power hungry, sexually immoral, lazy or can't keep their temper.

One day one of our preschoolers got mad at me. She looked up at me with her hands on her hips and said,

"Dad, you are making me so mad, I'm about to lose my temperature."

As the youngest brother in my family, I felt I had a lot to live up to, in my mind at least. One of my brothers had made a name for himself playing football. I idolized him for it, and so, I started playing football when I was eight years old. My older brother, who was eight years older than me, took an interest in me and became my coach. I soon learned I did not have to be big, I just had to hit harder than everyone else. I did unbelievably well. So much so that I became the team captain on my Junior High team, even though I wasn't the quarterback (I can't throw worth a darn). I began to know how to turn on the aggressive side of things. But something else happened; I was no longer able to control my temper. One day I got mad at a water hose at work, so I kicked it. I broke the water faucet clean off the wall. The water drenched me in half a second as it shot out of the broken pipe like a fire hydrant. To make matters worse it was winter and barley 30 degrees out. I knew right then I had to quit football, because it was cultivating an ungodly character in me. I looked stupid, I felt stupid and the Spirit was calling from inside me that I was all wet, and He had something better for me. You see, at that time I knew I was called to full time ministry.

Football was something I loved and was passionate about, so much so that even after I left, I couldn't watch a game because it aroused aggression within me. Football is not evil, but it was for me, because it changed my character into something that was not honoring to God.

As a young man knowing I was letting my temper become part of my life scared me. In particular, because I had once been on the receiving end of a youth leader I admired, who one day gave full vent to his temper. I received what I hoped never to give to someone else. I understood that my temper was a big deal to God, that I was not to feed it, and that I should do the things that would increase the fruit of the Spirit in me.

The apostle Peter struggled from time to time with letting unhealthy emotions come to the surface. I think this is why we all love him; we see his weakness and can relate. But the truth of the matter is we probably would have had a hard time around him before the Holy Spirit took control. Peter did have passion, but even Christ had to let Peter go through some suffering in order to bring him to a place that honored God. Peter was used by God even though he had a lot of work to do on his character, so look at what he writes:

"For this very reason make every effort to add to your faith, goodness; and to goodness, knowledge; and to knowledge, self-control and to self-control, perseverance; and to perseverance, godliness; and to godliness, brotherly kindness; and to brotherly kindness, love. For if you possess these qualities in increasing measure, they will keep you from being ineffective and unproductive in your knowledge of our Lord Jesus Christ. But if anyone does not have theme he is nearsighted and blind, and has forgotten that he has been cleansed from his past sins" (2 Peter 1:5—9).

There are several lists of Godly character in the Bible which carry the understanding that these attributes should not only be evident in our lives, but also we should be working on increasing their measure. If we do not, we will be ineffective and unproductive in our Christian lives.

Target Practice

Here is the practice I would like you to do. It is a bit humbling, but hey, it will help you work on that too. Go to someone who knows you well and will tell you the truth. Hopefully by now you have a mentor you are in a discipleship relationship with. Have them rate you on your character from 1-10. 10 being that they see Christ in you. You could do it yourself, but the reality is you probably don't see what others see in you. Then take one or two of the low ones and start to look for ways you could increase your character. Pray the Spirit would open opportunities to show himself through you. The lists below are some traits of Godly character (I did not list the repeats in other verses).

1. Galatians 5:22- Love, joy, peace, patience, kindness, goodness faithfulness, gentleness, self-control
2. Colossians 3:12–compassion, humility, bear with each other, forgiveness
3. 1 Timothy 3:1–above reproach, temperate, respectable, hospitable, not quarrelsome, not greedy, not overbearing, not given to drunkenness,
4. 2 Peter 1:5–perseverance, godliness, brotherly kindness,

Chapter 25

WHAT THE FATHER DESIRES
◎

Yet a time is coming and has now come when the true
worshipers will worship the Father in spirit and truth
for they are the kind of worshipers the Father seeks.
John 4:23

Y ou may be thinking to yourself, "What does worship
have to do with Godly character?" There was a part of
me that wondered this too, where did worship really fit in
to the whole list. It is part of our seeking Biblical wisdom,
because the more we know and fear God, there is a definite
draw to worship. Worship fits in with growing faith in some
ways too, for without faith there would be no worship. It
plays a huge part in balanced priorities, because loving God
first and foremost means He is who we worship. Later we'll
see sacrificial service is all about worship, but I cannot help
but believe that it starts with Godly Character. Character is an

outpouring of the heart and godly character is an outpouring of the Holy Spirit in your heart. Without the Spirit there is no true worship. The Father does not care about religious acts, but a true outward flow of the heart, in other words, a worshiper who worships in spirit and truth.

I hope you can see why I put it here. Out of all the five, worship and character start with the same thing, the outpouring of our heart. If the fruit of the Spirit is love, wouldn't it include our love for God, and isn't worship an outpouring of our love? What we love we pursue, what we pursue is an expression of worship.

Worship is often confused with the time of singing during a church service. Worship is a lot more than that. In some ways, the whole pursuit of spiritual maturity in this book is worship. It too can become a religious act, and no longer worship, if we do not pursue it in the strength of the Spirit nor are true to our hearts as we come before a mighty and holy God. Worship includes every area of the way we live our life.

If you are struggling to spend time in worship before God, this is a sign that something is not right. Now I'm not talking about times when the style of music, or how it is played, or even the volume is different than how you would prefer. Yes, these elements may make it hard for you to express your love to the Lord. But times like these are not the real issue. The times I'm talking about are when you are in control of your environment, and you still have a hard time expressing your love for the Lord, because this points to an issue of the heart.

156

For me, I worship best in mountain solitude. At my last camp I pitched my tent at over seven thousand feet. At meal time I sat on a ridge that overlooked a valley filled with streams, hills and prairies. To one side, a few mountain goats grazed on a sheer cliff that fell straight to the valley floor one thousand feet below. As I sat and watched the clouds roll by I felt like my heart was going to burst. The awe of God was everywhere to be seen. This scene showed His glory in a way I could never fully express, and in that moment His love for me was overwhelming.

We are all wired differently. While being in the solitude of the wilderness speaks to my heart, it only scares others. I love to worship with the voices of thousands but I have to close my eyes because the people are a distraction. I know of some that come to a place of worship as they spend time studying and researching through the Bible. And there are those who love to worship through the traditions of the church.

The question is do you get excited about God and do you seek out those times and places to express your worship to Him? If not then have you put out the Spirit's fire? There should be a longing to worship God for how He has redeemed you.

Target Practice

Find some time to get a way and express your love to the Lord. Listen to music, walk through a park or climb a mountain. Create a piece of art, sit and write a letter to the Lord. Visit a church that is known for their worship. Do something that will put you in a right place to express your heart, and make it a habit. I warn you if you cannot express your heart to the Lord, something is wrong and it is time to seek help.

PART 6:

SACRIFICIAL SERVICE

Chapter 26

DEDICATION

◎

*Therefore I urge you, brothers, in view of God's mercy,
to offer your bodies as living sacrifices, holy and
pleasing to God, this is your spiritual act of worship.*
Romans 12:1

I n the last chapter we talked about true worship. I love
Romans 12:1, because it cuts to the chase; your life is your
true act of worship. It just makes sense to me that we are living
sacrifices. Jesus said we have to die to ourselves. Paul said he
considered himself crucified with Christ and the life he now
lives is for Christ.[30]

We are called to totally surrender to Jesus' Lordship in our
lives; to put to death our old nature with its desires which are
killing us spiritually, because they are in direct conflict with
what God desires for our lives. This sacrifice comes in the form

of us offering our lives to God. He will not take it from us; we must be willing to lay it down ourselves.

A living sacrifice is simply us living for Christ, and it is a sacrifice. I look through the Old Testament and the truth is worship hardly ever came without sacrifice. For example, in 2 Samuel 24, David went out to worship the Lord. Upon finding the place he was to worship, he offered the land owner a fair price for the land and the items he needed to worship the Lord. The land owner wished to give them to him because he was the king, but David refused because he would not sacrifice to the Lord that which did not cost him. David understood that God cared little about what is given in comparison to how it is given.

Sacrificial service is simply living out what God has called us to do willingly. It comes in two parts. One part is motivated by the love we have for the Father. We desire to show love because we have come to a place where we know His love for us. The second is a desire to sacrifice as a statement of our dedication to the Father, Son, and Holy Spirit. True dedication always comes with sacrifice. Look at any athlete, look at anything that calls for dedication and you will see sacrifice. You simply cannot be dedicated to something if you are not willing to sacrifice. The moment you say, "That will cost me too much," is the moment you've reached the limit of your dedication. Peter was dedicated to his friend Jesus and willing to fight for him. He even took out a sword and was ready to take on the mob that came to arrest Jesus. But, when Jesus was not willing to fight, that was more dedication to God's will than Peter could give, and in the end he denied knowing Jesus altogether.

When I was sixteen I took a job moving irrigation pipe for the summer on a cattle ranch in the heart of Washington. My brother was a hired hand there and I thought this would be a great way to spend time with him, plus make some money. I was in no way ready for how much dedication it was going to take. I moved pipe from sun up to sunset every single day with a half day off on Sundays. I did the math and came to realize that I was only making about two dollars an hour, and that this was hard work. I knew I could have made more money back home, plus have time to hang out with my friends. Twelve weeks was going to kill me. When I talked to my brother he reminded me that I had said I was willing to do the job and that the integrity of my word was on the line. Plus, he thought that it would put him in a bad light, since he got me the job. I finished that summer, not for the money but because of my love and dedication to my brother. I was determined that I could not let him down.

Sacrificial service reveals itself through good works and generosity. Our understanding of good works is a messed up deal to say the least. Every religion out there calls for some sort of "good works" in order to obtain whatever they are shooting for. For the church, we hold that our good works do nothing for our salvation because it is by grace we are saved. But many slide into the same boat the Galatians did; which was, although they began with the power of the Spirit, they tried to obtain the goal of maturity through living out the Law, or through good works. Paul says that they had become bewitched and were fools.[31] The Law consists of rules and morality that come from the teachings of the Old Testament. These things are good and are not opposed to God, but we will never be able to live up to the standard. And that is the point. They are there in order for us to realize God calls for holiness and we will never qualify. So we need a Savior; someone who can meet the standard of the Law and intercede for us. Similarly, good works, if done as a means to meeting the standards established by the Law in order to please God, fall into the same category as the Galatians; we just can't do or be enough in order to be as holy as God.

There is a different type of good works that is sweet to God. It is the things we do as an expression of the heart. Because we are loved and forgiven we love and forgive others. Because we are blessed in spirit we bless others with what we have. Because we have been freed, we try to help others find freedom. It is not motivated by the thought, "This is what I must do to be a follower of Christ;" but rather, it comes from our dedication to follow Christ.

There is more to it than just dedication because we have experienced love from our Heavenly Father. It has a lot to do with the love we have because the Holy Spirit is at work in us. To do something because you should, misses the mark all over again. The stronger the Holy Spirit grows in your life, the more you will have love for others. Love is the motivator that should be our foundation to all that we do for others. The famous chapter that we all hear at weddings, 1Corinthians 13, lays it out pretty clearly that anything we do that is not because of love is pointless and holds no value. It is nothing but religious works which mean nothing.

Now think about it, it really is simple; it is the understanding of God's love that sets us free as we live in that wisdom. It is the holding on to love that gives us peace and trust to step out in faith. It is the guidance of God's love that helps us balance our priorities according to His will. It is love that is produced in us through the Spirit, and it is the expression of love that others see and praise God for.

It is possible to be generous and to have a life full of good works but if love is not at the heart of what we do, these things are only imposters and have nothing to do with spiritual maturity. For if they are not motivated by love for others or God, then they are done only out of love for ourselves and recognition from others. This is why Jesus says in Matthew 6:1, "Be careful not to practice your righteousness in front of others to be seen by them. If you do, you will have no reward from your Father in heaven." It is the "before men" part that gets us in trouble, for God wants our service to draw people to Him, not to glorify us.

Target Practice

How hard are you willing to push yourself for God? Are you willing to do a job without being appreciated? Are you willing to give beyond what you can, if asked? Will you serve at a task that is dirty and disgusting? Will you love those that you struggle with? It is time to ask God to help you push yourself.

Chapter 27

MADE FOR A PURPOSE
◎

*[Leadership of the church was given] to prepare
God's people for works of service so that the body
of Christ may be built up...From him the whole body
joined and held together by every supporting liga-
ment, grows and builds itself up in love as each part
does its work.* Ephesians 4:12, 16

E phesians chapter 4 describes what the church is supposed to be doing. Leadership is not given just to gather
a crowd and put on a show, impart some wisdom or encouragement and send the people on their way again. We are to do
our best to help the church find their place in the greater body
of Christ, for we all have a purpose that God has prepared for
us to do. It is not until we know and are doing the things that
God has for us that we truly become mature in Christ."For
it is by grace you have been saved, through faith—and this

is not from yourselves, it is the gift of God not by works, so that no one can boast. For we are God's handiwork, created in Christ Jesus to do good works, which God prepared in advance for us to do" (Ephesians 2:8-10).

You see, these verses are a big deal because they speak about a plan God has for each of us. These plans are not all the same. No, they are designed for us as unique individuals, plans and a purpose God has put together for us to bring about His glory and kingdom. Now part of the plan includes your finding victory in the five areas of spiritual maturity. One of which is focused on doing the things God has called you to. These good works are not our salvation but rather an expression of our love to Him because He saved us by grace.

If you think there is really nothing God would have you do for Him you are wrong and are not doing your part as a part of the body of Christ. Every believer regardless of background, age, sex, education or anything else you think may disqualify you, have been qualified simply by becoming a follower of Christ. In 1 Corinthians 12, Paul goes into great detail about the body. It is almost a rant, if there is such a thing in the Bible. As you read it, you start to get lost in trying to keep ears and eye and all the other parts straight. He talks about position and function, parts that are weaker or non-presentable, but how all of these parts should have no division and how we are to care for each part. The main point is that you are a part, and God has arranged us as He wanted.

Now I don't know how to make the case any stronger than you are to be doing the thing God has called you to. If you are not looking for what it is God has called you to, then you are missing out, missing out on the incredible joy and peace that comes from seeing God work in and through you as He touches others around you.

I was in fulltime ministry by the time I was eighteen. Since then, there has only been one period of six months that I was not in ministry, during which time I was trying to determine what God wanted us to do. Both Sacha and I could hardly stand it. It's not that ministry isn't hard, to be honest, there are times I hate it. The pressure and stress can be high at times. If it was just putting on a weekly gathering that would be a piece of cake. No it is the burden of all the people that you love and what they go through. The worst is when they turn their frustrations toward you and try to take you down. It is the Judas kiss when friends you love decide to do their best to hate you. At times like that I rest on the fact that God has called me to this ministry. You see regardless of the pain and suffering that comes there is no greater place to be than in the will of God. That six months being out of ministry was one of the most frustrating times of our life. We didn't see God moving in others, or God moving around us; it felt pointless. Not that God didn't use that time, but we knew we weren't being used and that is a place I never wish to go back to.

Now to be used by God does not mean you have to go into fulltime ministry, unless God has called you to. It does not even mean you have to work in the ministries of the church. Don't put a box around what God has called you to. The main thing is to start moving and doing the things God has put on your heart. Until you do you will struggle in many ways because you are not walking in what God has created you for. You will struggle for purpose if you are not carrying out the purpose God has for you.

Target Practice

When was the last time you felt God used you to help someone? Or, when was the last time you were full of joy or energy doing something? Are you spending any time looking for an opportunity to help; to show Gods love to others? Are you doing what you were created for?

Chapter 28

FINDING YOUR PURPOSE
◎

But in fact God has arranged the parts of the body, every one of them just as He wanted them to be. If they were all one part where would the body be? As it is there are many parts, but one body. 1 Corinthians 12:18-20

God has created us all unique and our uniqueness shows God's incredible glory. What He has created for you to do is going to be just as unique as you are. There is not much point in filling out a questionnaire to help you come up with what God is calling you to. Not that they are bad, so to speak. They might get you thinking, but I believe you need to start a journey of discovery which will lead you to the great reaches of God's love for you.

Let's start with the obvious. What do you have a heart for, what grips your emotions when you see or hear about it? Is there something you are drawn toward? It could be a people group, people of a certain age, a circumstance of life someone is in, etc. Or it could be more task-driven, a project that you feel you could do or something that you love to teach or talk about. There are so many things that could be pulling on your heart. If there is nothing that motivates you or that you enjoy doing, you need to check your pulse. If you still have a heart-beat then God has a purpose for you. I think if there is nothing that moves you, something is not healthy and perhaps you may be fighting depression.

There are four things to consider about the desire of your heart.

(1) Are you seeking God and His kingdom and glory for Him, or is it a selfless desire that you know is not from God. If it is not from God, run from it. If you're not sure, ask God to reveal it to you. He will. Remember to have a call on your life and do nothing about it is not OK with God. "What the righteous desire will be granted" (Proverbs 10:24).

(2) What can you do now that brings you closer to following your heart. Many times people have this grand dream of changing the world but they miss the first step. If you have a big dream, that is a call. You must start at step one. Before becoming the next Mother Teresa, consider just visiting your local hospital. Before becoming the next Billy Graham, talk to your neighbor. What I'm saying is this, do what is in front of you now, and see what God does with that. Be faithful with the small things first. "You have been faithful with a few things; I will put you in charge of many things" (Matthew 25:21).

(3) It is your burden, not everyone else's. What God has created for you to do is not for your pastor or church leadership to fulfill, it is for you to fulfill. God has laid it on your heart to do these things. Yes, invite people to come along. You never know what God will turn into a movement, so share your passion with whoever will listen. But don't become discouraged because others don't share your passion. If what you desire takes a team and you don't have one, remember, do what you can now. Don't use the excuse no one will help. Sometimes people need to see it happening before they get involved. It is your calling; follow it as Jesus sets the way.

(4) Don't give up, try something and if it doesn't work try it a different way or in a different place. You do not know God's timing, but if you are not willing to do your part you will never see God's timing. Now I'm not saying that you need to push so hard as to make things happen. Chances are if you do this, you will not be living with balanced priorities. Know there are times you will need to have open doors. But you should be checking the doors from time to time to see if they are locked. If God has shown you what is to come in advance, it is to give you hope. There will be times along the journey when you will question, "Where God or what is is God doing?" That is why He has shown you in advance so that you will remember His promises and push through regardless of the circumstances. But faith is stepping out when called to move. "Now the Jordan is at flood stage all during the harvest. Yet as soon as the priest who carried the ark reached the Jordan and their feet touched

the water's edge the water from upstream stopped flowing" (Joshua 3:15-16). Flood stage is pretty much a shut door, but when their feet touched the water, when they went as far as they could go, God did a miracle so they could do what they were called to do.

If God has made you unique, then He has something that fits who you are. That does not mean that it won't push you out of your comfort zone from time to time. But, if you put yourself in a place that's not your fit, you will not have the strength to do well or the joy to encourage others. Your passion will become depression; willingness will become obligation; an expression of love will become an act of religion. Get the point? Know yourself so you know your fit.

There was a gal who stepped into our Thursday kitchen ministry. She was great. Not only could she cook, she had run a commercial kitchen before. It was a joy to have our Thursday night meal in good hands. There was only one problem. She was by herself. The problem wasn't that she was overwhelmed by the work and needed help, but rather she was a people person, and as time went by she began to hate the job because it meant being by herself. Everyone appreciated her work, she was skilled at it, it was not a time issue; it simply was lonely for her and not a good fit. I should have seen it sooner, but by the time I did, it was too late.

There are a lot of personality tests out there. The point is: do you know yourself? Are you a people person or a strong leader; a detail person or do you love helping out behind the scene? Often people seem to think they need to be someone else in order to be used. Understand this, everyone is needed. If you think you are unfit, remember God uses the weak things of this world to glorify Himself. We are just to be faithful.

Target Practice

There is a lot to do under this one. But I would start by asking God for a dream, a burden that would take hold of your heart. This is going to take some prayer and time if you aren't there yet. In the meantime take some personality tests and discover who God has made you to be. Look, or even ask your mentor or a church leader where your personality and talents could be used. I would even take some time to look at your spiritual gifts and work on strengthening them through serving others.

Do not get bogged down in confusion. Try to serve some-where, and if it is not a good fit try something else within the church or outside of the church. I would challenge you to talk to a spiritual friend or mentor about what God is laying on your heart. Accountability is a great motivator.

Chapter 29

DO YOU LOVE OTHERS
◎

Do nothing out of selfish ambition or vain conceit,
but in humility consider others better than yourselves.
Philippians 2:3

We often talk about the Golden Rule, or treating others the way we wish to be treated. But Jesus takes it a step further by demonstrating through his sacrifice how we are to consider others better than ourselves. Don't forget the rest of the verse in Philippians. I did not put it at the beginning of the chapter for fear you would glaze over them. Basically they say our attitude should be the same as that of Jesus, "Rather, he made himself nothing by taking the very nature of a servant, being made in human likeness" (Philippians 2:7). This is what Christ came to do. He said himself; he did not come to be served, but to serve. We cannot run away from this one. If we are to be like Christ, and if this is a measure of our spiritual maturity, then we are not to just have a heart for others, we are to live a life that serves others.

Our daughter, Naomi served in Haiti on a mission trip a year after it had been devastated by the most recent earthquake. She was overwhelmed by the joy in the hearts of the people, their praise for God despite all they had lost. Her team had to return from Haiti early because of cholera, and finished out their time by cleaning out a hoarder's home. This woman died without emergency responders being able to rescue her, because her many possessions made it impossible to reach her. Her addiction to things literally killed her.

This had a profound impact on my daughter. Not just in experiencing these two extremes, but also because she lived out her summer serving people. This was life changing for her. One of the greatest benefits we often don't realize is that when we sacrifice to serve other people our biggest reward is the change in our own life.

When my wife visited her parents in Kolkata, India, she was changed forever as she stepped over malnourished moms sleeping on the sidewalks, their babies clinging to their chests. As she met the women who had been rescued from the train tracks and who now had homes, she was blown away with how thankful and proud they were of their new homes. Their homes were no bigger than our bathroom and the impact on my wife was profound. When you serve those who are deeply in need, you will be changed. Suddenly your wish list will seem petty, your value systems will be redefined and your contentment will grow.

One of my friends at church has me programmed in his phone as servant Mark. He thinks it is funny, but it always makes me think, "Am I truly living up to that holy calling?" I wish that I could say that I was one of the greats in the kingdom, but I am far from it. You see the greats in the kingdom of heaven will be the servant of all. I would doubt I'm even middle class. We all have things to work on, but this one hits me hard. I myself by nature, sin nature that is, am not a servant. But I eagerly desire to grow in this area.

I believe that this part of sacrificial service is also linked to our having godly character, in the sense of being filled with love for others. Let's faces it, love is the motivator to becoming a servant, and how else do we increase our love for each other than to consider one another better than ourselves? It is also part of balanced priorities that we live intentionally towards others as we die to self.

Target Practice

Begin by asking God to open your eyes to the needs of others. If something comes up don't just forget about it, write it down and put it on the calendar. I have found that if it is not on the calendar it will not happen. At the same time I'm sure that there are several places in the church and community that can use a selfless servant. Find one that tugs at your heart strings and get involved. Pray about going on a mission trip to a needy part of the world; it will do more for you than you can imagine.

Chapter 30

GIVING BEYOND YOURSELF

◎

Do not forget to do good and to share with others, for with such sacrifices God is pleased. Hebrews 13:16

G enerosity is an expression of the heart; we can be generous with our time, stuff, money, all sorts of things. But true generosity always calls for a bit of sacrifice. When there is no sacrifice there is no true generosity. Sharing your excess may supplement what is lacking to someone else but it does little for you. And believe it or not, I'm not concerned about what others may get from your giving; God knows what they need and He is their provider. I don't say that flippantly, I know what it is to live on what God alone can provide. For the majority of my working career, I have never earned a paycheck from those I ministered to, and yet God has always provided.

No, I'm concerned with what is going on in you. Generosity is not the amount, but the sacrifice. A couple of years ago we wanted to take our whole family on a mission trip to Thailand before they left the home and went off to college. For a family of five, this loomed as a daunting task and was far beyond our financial resources. So the girl's all sent out prayer letters and hoped that someone would help us financially with what we could not do. We have great friends who were very generous. For a trip that not only gave us an unbelievable family memory, but cemented in them some spiritual things that will shape their lives to come.

One of those spiritual things happened to my youngest. She had a younger friend who had been saving for a year for an I-pod; she decided to give her money to my Rebecca. It was not the biggest gift she got, but it was the sacrifice and her friend's generosity that got her attention. It is an act that is still at work in Rebecca's heart molding her own thoughts about generosity, love, and sacrificial service.

There is a weird story Jesus tells about a shrewd servant in Luke 16 you don't hear much about, because it is a little confusing. You see this servant was going to get fired so he went to his master's debtors. Knowing that he was not going to have a place to live soon he tells them to forget about paying half of their debt. He fixes the books, so that when he is thrown out he could go and stay with the people he helped. The confusing part is he is commended for this. What Jesus was getting at was through this story is, we are not going to be here too long and that we are to use our master's (God's) resources to befriend and love on others, which is really, loving God, so that when we get to heaven we will be welcomed home. Not that generosity is a way of salvation. But generosity leads to a greater reward in heaven.

The Bible tells us in several places that we are to store up treasures in heaven by being generous to others, and by guarding ourselves from what our heart desire. One of the ways we do this is by giving on a regular schedule, our tithes to the church. It helps us to remember that God is our provider, and to not hold on to riches. As well, we are told to share with others who lead the church and that this is our duty to them, for it is how God designed it.

The thing about generosity is God calls us to it. Knowing that it will take a sacrifice to do it, but then He promises to be generous to us. Giving to us according to the measure we have given. Plus, think about God being generous to us; you can't lose. Know that I'm not for the prosperity doctrine, the idea that "I give therefore God *has* to give me more." No, that does not fly. But God does not lie. He will give what you need so that you can abound in every good work. Remember this.

"Whoever sows sparingly will also reap sparingly and whoever sows generously will also reap generously. Each man should give what he has decided in his heart to give, not reluctantly or under compulsion, for God loves a cheerful giver. And God is able to make all grace abound to you, so that in all things at all

times, having all that you need, you will abound in every good work" (2 Corinthians 9:6—8).

I think it is important for us to understand that worship does call for sacrifice, and generosity is a part of it. One of the greatest challenges I have encountered in recent years has come from reading where Paul tells the church to increase or grow in several areas for example, love. Another area we are to grow in is our generosity. Our giving is to be consistent. After praying about it and being motivated by the testimonies in the book *Radical*[32], I decided that I would add a percentage to my giving every year on my birthday (I'm not planning on living too long). The first few years our paycheck actually decreased, but we have been able to do it and the blessing of helping out others has added more to my life than the money ever could. I don't tell you this to brag, I tell you this because when I heard it from someone else, it encouraged me to grow in my generosity.

Target Practice

Simply, are you giving to the church what you should? If not, do it.

Don't be that person that has to split the bill 50/50. Step out and pay the whole thing as a way to love on your friends.

If you are a slave to debt you need to get out, because you are missing out on so much that God would love to throw your way. Go get help, stop making excuses, get online, talk to someone, work on it, and make it a priority. If you can't do it, you have a real problem that needs to be dealt with before it destroys your relationships.

Ask your family where they would like to be generous to someone and do it together. If money has a hold on you, read the book, *Treasure Principle*[33]. I have one in the bathroom and read it whenever finances get me down. It helps me refocus.

We often get confused thinking we are accomplishing these things for God, but the truth of the matter is that God is more concerned with what He is accomplishing in us, through our service.

SIGHTED IN

◎

From the days of John the Baptist until now, the kingdom of heaven has been forcefully advancing, and forceful men lay hold of it. Matthew 11:12

A few years ago Outdoorsmen Church initiated an annual spring gopher hunt. Men of all ages look forward to this crazy day of gopher annihilation. The morning starts with a breakfast together where each team tries to figure out their competitor's strategies. I always go out with my bow, but had the hilarious privilege of videoing my team's first year hunt with their rifles. At the end of the video I had to make the disclaimer, "No gophers were hurt in the making of this movie." As the teams brought in their harvest, I was blown away that it was not just my team who had done poorly. The harvest rate was shockingly low for the whole event. As we started our next activity, target shooting, it became apparent what the problem was. Every guy that stepped up to shoot was way off target, except for the gopher hunt winner of the morning. He was the only guy who had sighted in his gun.

What is interesting to me is that the guys would have been sighted in had it been elk season. Only a greenhorn would not have known what it took to be ready for the *big* hunt for the year. What was different is that these were just rodents and the men didn't feel the need to prepare. I'm afraid that when it comes to spiritual maturity we can be a lot like these guys. We read all about it, but aren't willing to put in the time and effort to make it a reality in our lives.

As I have said to grow in spiritual maturity and to have a victorious walk with Christ, it will take a daily surrendering of your life to Him. We must in His word daily. If you are new to reading the Bible start in one of his four Gospels. Use the S.O.A.P. method of Scripture, Observation, Application and Prayer. Write down what you are observing, have questions about or need to apply. Record your prayer requests so that your faith is built as you see God answer in miraculous ways.

Not everything is going to change overnight but the more you live with intentionality the more you will have a victorious life in Christ. Focus on one thing that has been revealed to you and find someone that you can meet with who will encourage you in this journey. In Hebrews 10:24-27, we read "And let us consider how we may spur one another on toward love and good deeds, not giving up meeting together, as some are in the habit of doing, but encouraging one another—and all the more as you see the Day approaching."

An accountability partner is an essential key; they help you see areas that you would otherwise miss. Discuss together the following five areas of spiritual maturity and make an intentional plan to grow together.

Biblical wisdom is evident in the decisions you make every day. To grow in this area we must be in God's word regularly, asking the Holy Spirit to teach us and reveal to us the changes we need to apply to our life.

Growing faith is seen through your peace as you trust God beyond what you can see in your circumstances. It reveals itself as you step out in what He calls you to do beyond your comfort zone.

Balanced Priorities are shown by having healthy relationships, with our relationship with God always having top priority. Our relationships with family, the church and unbelievers are only healthy if our relationship with God is strong. We must live with intentionality and a love for others above ourselves.

Our godly character is an overflow of the heart. Our true nature is often revealed when we are under pressure. The Holy Spirit changes character as it produces fruit in our life. Keeping in step with the spirit and dealing with the things that are of our old nature develops our character to be more like Christ.

Sacrificial service is evident in our generosity and the good works that we do to show God's love. Sacrifice is a part of our worship and we are told to present ourselves as a living sacrifice to our Lord. He has created us unique and with a special purpose that we may glorify him as we live a life of purpose in the body of Christ. We need to actively seek where God would have us love on others through the gifts and abilities that He has given us.

If you were to have come to our gopher hunt the next year, you would have been surprised at the harvest. The men quickly learned that they didn't want to be embarrassed again. They worked hard to be prepared for success. This book has given you the tools to "aim small, miss small." The question is will you answer the call to be fully committed to spiritual maturity?

ENDNOTES
◎

CHAPTER 1: SPIRITUALLY DEAD OF SPIRITUALLY RETIRED

1. 2 Timothy 3:5.

CHAPTER 2: THE PETER PAN MENTALITY

2. J.M. Barrie, *Peter and Wendy (UK: Charles Scribner's Sons, 1911)*.

3. Brainy Quote, "E.E. Cummings Quotes: 2001, " Brainy Quote.http://www.brainyquote.com/quotes/quotes/e/eecummin161593.html (Accesses December 12, 2014).

4. John 10:10.

5. *The Patriot.* Directed by Roland Emmerich. 2000; Columbia Pictures Corporation.

6. Proverbs 29:18a. The Holy Bible, King James Version, KJV. Dallas, TX: Brown Books Publishing, 2004.

7. The Barna Group, "Many Churchgoers and Faith Leaders Struggle to Define Spiritual Maturity: May 11, 2009," Barna Group. https://www.barna.org/barna-update/faith-spirituality/264-many-church-goers-and-faith-leaders-struggle-to-define-spiritual-maturity (Accessed December 10, 2014).

8. Ibid.

CHAPTER 3: GROWING UP

9. The earliest evidence located by *Quote Investigator* was printed in a syndicated gossip column based in New York on June 13, 1937. The statement was ascribed to Paul Terry who was the founder of the Terrytoons animation studio. Garson, "Whenever I Feel the Urge to Exercise I Lie Down Until It Goes Away: June, 2012," Quote Investigator.http://quoteinvestigator.com/2012/06/09/urge-to-exercise/ (Accessed December 10, 2014).

10. John 10:10. The Holy Bible: English Standard Version, ESV. IL: Crossway, 2002.

CHAPTER 4: THE POWER FOR LIFE CHANGE

11. Albert Lang, "New Report: Montana has the Seventh Lowest Adult Obesity Rate in Nation: September 2014," Trust for American's Health. http://healthyamericans.org/reports/obesity2014/?stateid=MT.(Accessed December 12, 2014).

12. 1 Corinthians 2:11a.

13. Galatians 2:11-14.
14. Acts10:9-16.

CHAPTER 5: DEFINING SPIRITUAL MATURITY

15. The Barna Group, "Many Churchgoers and Faith Leaders Struggle to Define Spiritual Maturity: May 11, 2009," Barna Group. https://www.barna.org/barna-update/faith-spirituality/264-many-church-goers-and-faith-leaders-struggle-to-define-spiritu-al-maturity (Accessed December 10, 2014).

CHAPTER 7: THE IMPOSTER

16. John 9:13-34.
17. Matthew 15:14.
18. John 12:8.

CHAPTER 8: APPLYING UNDERSTANDING

19. *Forest Gump*. Directed by Robert Zemeckis. 1994; Paramount Pictures.

CHAPTER 13: WHO ARE YOU PURSUING?

20. Luke 6:44.

CHAPTER 14: LEAP OF FAITH

21. Matthew 13:1—23.
22. Revelation 21:8.

CHAPTER 16: IT'S NOT ABOUT YOU

22. Matthew 22:37.

23. 2 Corinthians 5:18.

23. Figure 1 shows how our priorities should be balanced between the four main relationships in our lives; starting with our relationship with God and ending with our relationships with unbelievers.

CHAPTER 17: RELATIONSHIP WITH GOD

24. Romans 8:31.

CHAPTER 19: RELATIONSHIP WITH BELIEVERS

25. Alan Smith "Christian Church Life–Where I Used To Go To Church: 2002." Surf In the Spirit. http://www.surfinthespirit.com/church/used-to-go.html (Accessed December 10, 2014).

26. Figure 2 shows the relationships we are to have with believers.

CHAPTER 20: RELATIONSHIP WITH UNBELIEVERS

27. Don Everts and Doug Schaupp, *I Once Was Lost: What Postmodern Skeptics Taught Us about Their Path to Jesus* (Downers Grove, Ill.: IVP Books, 2008).

CHAPTER 23: LIFE IS PAIN

28. *The Princess Bride*. Directed by Rob Reiner. 1988; 20th Century Fox.

29. *Sands of Iwo Jima*. Directed by Alan Dawn. 1949; Republic Pictures.

CHAPTER 26: DEDICATION

30. Galatians 2:20.
31. Galatians 3:1-6.

CHAPTER 30: GIVING BEYOND YOURSELVES

31. David Platt, *Radical: Taking Back Your Faith from the American Dream* (Colorado Springs, Colo.: Multnomah Books, 2010).
32. Randy C. Alcorn, *The Treasure Principle* (Sisters, Or.: Multnomah Publishers, 2001)

ABOUT THE AUTHOR

◎

Mark Hasenyager is the founding pastor of Outdoorsmen Church, which focuses on breaking down the barriers preventing Montanans from seeking Christ. After moving to Montana, it didn't take long to discover that Montanans are passionate about hunting and the great outdoors. Mark has always loved being in the outdoors and enjoying what God has created. It was a natural fit to connect his passion for the outdoors with his passion for Christ and to bring others to know Him. In March of 2013, Mark founded Multiply Northwest, a church planting center that develops effective spiritual leaders to start culturally relevant new works in the Northwest. Find out more at www.outdoorsmenchurch.com and www.multiplynorthwest.com. Email him at aimsmall@outdoorsmenchurch.com.

OUTDOORSMEN CHURCH
◎

Western Montana abounds with opportunities to enjoy the outdoors. Whether it is hunting, fishing, white water rafting, rock climbing, snowmobiling, skiing, camping or hiking. Unfortunately, this has made it very hard to reach the un-churched. To tell someone, "Jesus loves you, and He wants you to give up every Sunday for the rest of your lives," has been a barrier for Montanans in seeking Christ. In 2005, God laid on their hearts a unique vision to begin a culturally relevant church plant based on a relational ministry approach. In the spring of 2005, Outdoorsmen Church began in the Hasenyager's home in Huson, MT, with church services on Thursday nights and a free BBQ before church. God has greatly used this unique style of ministry.

The services are incredibly relaxed, with a "come in your jeans and don't be afraid of spilling the coffee" philosophy. Services are midweek, with a free BBQ dinner, followed by contemporary worship and solid Biblical teaching relevant to our community. This unique church has had God's blessing on it from the start. Seventy percent of the church's growth has come through new believers and it quickly became apparent we would have to have an intentional discipleship process in order to raise up spiritually mature believers.

In March of 2013, the Lord laid on our hearts the vision of starting a training center to develop church planters. Multiply Northwest trains interns who are developed to reach the un-churched of the Northwest through solidly biblical, culturally relevant churches. Our church planting center provides weekly one on one coaching for leadership development, discipleship training and mentoring. Beyond this we also provide classroom training where we cover Biblical theology, church management, planting strategy and speaking. At our campus we provide hands on ministry experience with children's ministry, preaching, small groups, youth ministry, event planning and more.

Find out more at www.outdoorsmenchurch.com or www. multiplynorthwest.com.

CPSIA information can be obtained
at www.ICGtesting.com
Printed in the USA
FSOW01n2153020215
4970FS